Computer-Output Microfilm:

Its Library Applications

WILLIAM SAFFADY

American Library Association
CHICAGO 1978

Library of Congress Cataloging in Publication Data

Saffady, William, 1944-
  Computer-output microfilm.

  Bibliography: p.
  1. Computer output microfilm devices--Library
applications. I. Title.
Z699.3.S23   025.3'028'54   78-18416
ISBN 0-8389-3217-7

This report was prepared for the
Council on Library Resources.

Printed in the United States of America

PURPOSE AND SCOPE OF THIS REPORT

This report is designed for library personnel, including systems analysts, administrators, and others who need an understanding of the latest developments in Computer-Output-Microfilm (COM) equipment, software, applications, and systems design. The report is divided into the following sections:

1. An introduction to the development of COM hardware and applications in science, business, and libraries.

2. A review of COM hardware and software, describing the latest developments in recording technologies, input preparation, and microform duplication.

3. An evaluation of COM as an alternative to line printers and real-time computer systems employing CRT's.

4. A review of factors influencing the design of COM applications from the user's viewpoint, including the choice of microform, reduction ratio, reading equipment, and retrieval coding.

5. A brief analysis of the relationship of COM to certain other technologies of interest to libraries.

Supplemental information on COM hardware, costs, standards, and services is presented in appendices.

The report reflects the state-of-the-art through January, 1978, subject to the following limitations:

1. Historically, libraries have been users rather than owners of COM recorders. It is expected that this will continue to be the case with the exception of a few major institutions, such as the Library of Congress. Consequently, the report omits discussion of some operational features, such as ease of film loading and effective throughput speed, which are of significance primarily to potential buyers of COM recorders.

2. Throughout the report, particular equipment is mentioned as representative of certain features. The list of equipment mentioned in such contexts is not necessarily exhaustive and inclusion does not imply endorsement.

3. In Appendix B, emphasis is placed on COM recorders currently available for sale in the United States. Recorders no longer manufactured and equipment available only in Europe are generally omitted.

TABLE OF CONTENTS

Page

GLOSSARY OF TERMS   1

INTRODUCTION   7
    Development of COM   7
    Library Applications   9
    COM for Micropublishing   12

COM HARDWARE AND SOFTWARE   16
  Non-Technical Summary   16
    The COM Recorder   16
    Data Preparation   18
  The COM Recorder   19
    Modes of Operation   19
    Recording Methods   23
    Forms Recording   32
  Input Preparation Requirements   34
    Tapes Accepted   34
    Tape Preparation   35
    The Subroutine Method   36
    Print-Tape Translation   41
    Minicomputer-controlled COM Recorders   43
    Data Preparation for On-Line Recording   45
    Emulation Software   45
  Output Capabilities   46
    Microforms Produced   46
    Effective Reduction Ratios and Internal Formats   47
    Alphanumeric vs Graphic Recording   55
  COM Duplication   56
    Duplicating Film Stocks   56
    Duplicating Equipment   60
  COM Service Bureaus   61

COM AS A COMPUTER OUTPUT ALTERNATIVE   63
  COM as Line Printer Replacement   63
    Recording Speed   63
    Economy   66
    Output Quality   74
    Printable Character Sets   75
    Type Face, Size, and Intensity   82
    Page Formatting   84
  COM vs On-Line Systems   86
    COM as an On-Line System Alternative   88
    COM in a Hybrid System   91
    COM as On-Line System Back-Up   93
  Limitations of COM   94

	Page
COM SYSTEMS DESIGN	96
Output Selection	96
Roll Microforms vs Microfiche	96
Low vs High Reduction	106
COM Display Equipment	110
Display Methods	110
Image Quality	116
General Engineering	117
Reader Size	119
Microforms Accepted and Magnification	120
Screen-Size and Orientation	122
Special Display Features	123
Human Factors in Reader Selection	124
Use Instruction	127
Cost	128
Reader/Printers	129
The Surrounding Environment	131
Retrieval Coding and Indexing	132
Eye-Legible Characters for Roll Microforms	133
Odometer Indexing	134
Image Count Marks (Blips)	136
Code-Lines	136
MIRAcode and Oracle Coding	138
Eye-Legible Microfiche Titling	142
Microfiche Indexing	144
LINKS TO OTHER SYSTEMS	147
Printing/Publishing	147
Computer-Input-Microfilm	148
REFERENCES	151
APPENDIX	
A. A General Formula for Determining Monthly COM Costs	158
B. COM Recorder Specification Summaries	160
C. Selected Standards Relevant to COM Recording	181
D. Companies Specializing in the Production of COM Catalogs for Libraries	184
E. Selected Additional Bibliography	186

LIST OF FIGURES

Page

1. Modes of COM Recorder Operation   20

2. Operation of an Off-Line COM Recorder   22

3. COM Recording by CRT Photography   25

4. Charactron Shaped Beam Tube used in DatagraphiX COM Recorders   26

5. Laser Beam COM Recording   30

6. A COM Form Slide   33

7. Formatting of Line Printer Records under DOS   38

8. The Subroutine Method of COM Input Preparation   39

9. The Print Tape Translation Method   42

10. Placement of 16mm COM Images   49

11. NMA Type 3, 24X COM Microfiche Format   51

12. NMA Type 5, 42X COM Microfiche Format   52

13. NMA Type 7, 48X COM Microfiche Format   53

14. Variations in COM Costs with Monthly Update Frequency   70

15. Variations in COM Costs with Number of Distribution Points   72

16. Variations in COM Costs with Report Length   73

17. Extended COM Character Set   77

18. Japanese Katakana Matrix   80

19. Scrolled Page Format   87

20. Autographics Reader showing Large 16mm Reel   98

21. 16mm Microfilm Cartridge   100

22. 16mm Microfilm Cassette   101

23. Panel-Type Filing for Microfiche   107

		Page
24.	Schematic Drawing of Front Projection Optical Path	112
25.	Front-Projection COM Reader	113
26.	Schematic Drawing of Rear Projection Optical Path	114
27.	Rear-Projection COM Reader	115
28.	ROM 3 Microform Viewer Showing Side-Mounted Index	135
29.	Image Count Marks	137
30.	Code-Line Indexing	139
31.	MIRAcode	140
32.	Microfiche Titling and Indexing	143

LIST OF TABLES

		Page
1.	Comparison of Line Printer and 24:1 COM Costs	68
2.	Comparison of Line Printer and COM Costs for Extended Character Set Work	81
3.	Comparison of Cartridge Roll Film and Microfiche Costs	103
4.	Comparison of COM Fiche Costs at 24:1 and 42:1 Reductions	109

GLOSSARY OF TERMS USED IN THIS REPORT

ALPHANUMERICS

A generic term for alphabetic characters, numeric digits, punctuation symbols, and special characters.

ARCHIVAL POTENTIAL

The ability of a processed microform to retain its original characteristics, and resist deterioration, over time, when properly stored.

ASCII

American Standard Code for Information Interchange; one of several coding schemes for the representation of digital data on magnetic tape or other machine-readable media; used widely by non-IBM computers.

BCD

Binary-Coded Decimal; one of several coding schemes for the representation of digital data on magnetic tape or other machine-readable media; used in second generation IBM computers such as the model 1401.

CAMERA ORIGINAL MICROFORM

The microfilm or microfiche that is produced by a source document camera or COM recorder, as opposed to microforms created by duplication.

CARTRIDGE

A plastic, single-core container for 16mm or 35mm microfilm. When mounted on an appropriate reader, microfilm from the cartridge is automatically threaded onto a take-up spool built into the reader itself. The microfilm passes out of the cartridge during use and must be rewound into the cartridge prior to removal from the reader.

CASSETTE

A plastic, double-core container for 16mm microfilm. Unlike a cartridge, a cassette encloses both the supply spool and take-up spool in a single housing. Cassettes require no film threading and can be removed from the reader at any time without rewinding.

1

CATHODE-RAY-TUBE (CRT)

A vacuum tube in which a narrow beam of electrons can
be moved about on a luminescent screen to form alphanumeric
characters or graphics. CRT displays are used in the
most prevalent method of COM recording.

CINE MODE

A method of image placement on roll microfilm in which
the lines of text within the microimages are perpendicular
to the edges of the film.

COMIC MODE

A method of image placement on roll microfilm in which
the lines of text within the microimages are parallel
to the edges of the film.

COMPUTER-INPUT-MICROFILM (CIM)

Technology concerned with converting human-readable
information on microfilm to machine-readable data
suitable for computer processing.

COMPUTER OUTPUT-MICROFILM (COM)

The end product of a process which converts, machine-
readable, computer-processable digital data to
human-readable textual or graphic information in
microform without first creating paper documents.

COM RECORDER

A device which produces computer-output-microfilm.

COM SOFTWARE

In COM applications, the programs necessary to format
and index data for recording on microfilm or microfiche.

COM TAPE

A specially-formatted tape containing machine instructions
and data to be recorded by an off-line COM recorder.

COM TRANSLATOR PROGRAM

A set of machine instructions designed to convert a
magnetic tape containing print records suitable for
output by a line printer into a magnetic tape containing
print records suitable for output by a COM recorder.

COMPUTER PERIPHERAL

A generic term for various machines used in combination
or in conjunction with a computer. Typical computer
peripherals include printers, card readers, CRT terminals,
tape readers, disk drives and COM recorders.

COMPUTER PRINTOUT PAGE

A sheet of paper, typically measuring eleven inches high
by fourteen inches wide, intended for use with computer
printers. Computer produced paper output is typically
printed on continuous fanfold form stock.

DIGITAL DATA

Alphabetic characters, numeric digits, or other symbols
or information represented by a dual-state condition
such as magnetized or demagnetized spots on tape, or
open or closed circuits.

DOT MATRIX

A rectangular array of dots forming alphanumeric
characters. In COM recording the dots are light
points on the face of a cathode-ray-tube.

EBCDIC

Extended Binary-Coded Decimal Interchange Code; one of
several coding schemes for digital data; used by IBM
System 360/370 computers.

EFFECTIVE REDUCTION RATIO

In COM recording, the ratio between a given linear dimension
of an imaginary document and the corresponding linear
dimension of a microimage. In most cases, the imaginary
document is an eleven by fourteen inch computer printout
page.

FORM SLIDE

A mechanism incorporated in many COM recorders. It
consists of a transparent piece of glass or film bearing
the image of a business form with blank spaces for variable
information. To emulate report production on pre-printed
form stock, the form slide is exposed to film while the
blank spaces are being filled in with the user's data.

GRAPHICS

Information in the form of pictorial representation, as
opposed to alphanumeric characters. For purposes of
COM recording, two types of graphics are distinguished:
1) scientific graphics, such as engineering drawings
and contour plots; and 2) business graphics, such as
bar charts, pie charts, and histograms.

LINE PRINTER

An impact-type paper printer in which an entire line of
characters is composed within the device prior to printing.

MACHINE-READABLE DATA

Data represented in coded form suitable for storage in
and processing by a machine such as a computer.

MAGNETIC TAPE

A reel of plastic or metallic tape with a ferrous oxide
coating upon which data can be recorded magnetically.

MICROFICHE

A rectangular sheet of film containing multiple micro-images
in a two-dimensional grid pattern of rows and columns.
The standard, and by far the most common, microfiche
size is 105 x 148mm (approximately four by six inches).

MICROFILM SERVICE BUREAU

An organization, typically a private business, which
creates microforms using a customer's own documents
or machine-readable data.

MICROFORM

A generic term for any information communication or
storage medium containing images too small to be read
without magnification.

MICROFORM DUPLICATION

The production of single or multiple microform copies
of a given microform; as, for example, in the production
of distribution copies from a master microfiche.

MICROIMAGE

An image, containing textual or graphic information,
too small to be read without magnification.

MICROPUBLISHING

The publication of information in microform for sale
or distribution to the public.

MINICOMPUTER

A computer typically distinguished from a large-scale
computer by size and/or price. A growing number of COM
recorders feature an attached minicomputer to reformat
magnetic tapes containing data originally intended for
printing onto paper.

OFF-LINE COM RECORDER

A stand-alone device which accepts appropriately-formatted
magnetic tapes containing the data to be recorded on
microfilm and embedded machine instructions. An off-line
COM recorder is not connected to, and therefore does not
operate under the control of, the computer on which the
tape was prepared. An off-line COM recorder may be
located remotely from the computer which produced the
data tape.

ON-LINE COM RECORDER

A COM recorder that is connected to a computer and operates
under its control. An on-line COM recorder receives the
data to be recorded directly from a computer, rather than
from a magnetic tape.

ON-LINE INFORMATION SYSTEM

An information system in which data maintained on disks,
drums, or other direct access storage devices can be
accessed by users at remote terminals.

OPTICAL CHARACTER RECOGNITION (OCR)

The use of photosensitive scanners to convert alphanumeric
characters to machine-readable form for computer processing.
The characters are typically typed or printed in a special
font designed for machine recognition.

ORIGINAL MICROPUBLISHING

The publication of previously unpublished material in microform.

READER

A projection device that magnifies microimages so they can be read with the unaided eye.

READER/PRINTER

A projection device that displays magnified microimages for reading and enables the user to make paper prints of the displayed images.

REAL-TIME INFORMATION SYSTEM

An information system in which data is changed to reflect transactions as they occur. In a real-time circulation system, for example, circulation transactions are posted to the file as items are checked out, thereby assuring the currency of data.

REEL MICROFILM

16mm or 35mm microfilm wound on a flanged plastic holder.

ROLL MICROFORM

A generic term for microfilm on reels, in cartridges, or in cassettes.

SOURCE DOCUMENT MICROPHOTOGRAPHY

The creation of microforms from paper documents, using cameras.

SUBROUTINE

In computer programming, a set of machine instructions or program, designed to perform a specific task and which is included as part of another program. In COM recording, subroutines can be utilized to format print records.

SECTION ONE

INTRODUCTION

Microform is a generic term for any information communication or storage medium containing images too small to be read without magnification. The images themselves, properly called <u>microimages</u> are, in the main, photographically produced and may contain textual or graphic information. Since the nineteenth century, microphotographic technology has permitted the creation of microimages from bound volumes, technical reports, office correspondence, and other source documents using cameras. By definition, this source document microphotography requires the prior existence of information in paper form. Over the last 20 years, however, a new method of microform creation has developed. The acronym <u>COM</u> denotes the product (computer-output-microfilm), the process (computer-output-microfilming), and the device (computer-output-microfilmer) that converts machine-readable,[*] computer-processable digital data[*] to human-readable textual or graphic information in microform <u>without first creating paper documents</u>.

Development of COM

The computer industry and computer users, as noted by Boyd (1973) in an excellent history of COM technology, have

---

[*] For definitions of terms marked with an asterisk, see glossary.

long been troubled by the disparity between processing speed and the slowness of input/output devices. The earliest COM units were developed during the 1950's as alternatives to slow mechanical plotters in scientific and technical applications requiring high-volume, high-resolution generation of computer graphics* such as contour plots, engineering drawings, maps, charts, and circuit diagrams. The performance of these early scientific COM units was often marginal, but users tolerated their limitations to gain recording speed.

Stromberg DatagraphiX developed the first business-application COM recorder, a specially-designed device, for the Social Security Administration in 1958. Production models for commercial applications appeared in the 1960's, but such applications developed slowly. Although an estimated 300 COM recorders were installed by 1968, Avedon (1969) reported that one-third of seventy-four users surveyed by the National Microfilm Association were applying COM to scientific problems. The early 1970's, however, saw a significant increase in non-scientific COM applications. Enders (1975) reports that the sale of COM viewing equipment -- estimated at ten thousand to fifteen thousand units through the late 1960's -- had more than doubled by the end of 1971. Robinson (1973) suggests the year 1972 as a turning point for COM acceptance in business applications. He attributes this to the introduction of lease plans tailored to user needs, new hardware options, and increased customer

confidence resulting from first steps toward standardization.
Quantor Corporation (1975), a COM manufacturer, estimates that
2,530 non-scientific recorders had been installed by 1975 with
an installed base of 7,630 predicted for 1980. International
Data Corporation, in a report by Ross (1976), projected COM's
share of the total U.S. computer output market, in terms of
number of pages, at twenty-four percent by 1979, up from
sixteen percent in 1974. This growth will undoubtedly be
stimulated by increased emphasis on economies in EDP operations,
together with the development of COM systems design for applications
requiring more than mere line printer replacement. Such potential
applications have been described by Harrison (1973, 1974),
Malabarba (1975), Neary (1976), and Neary, Coyle, and Avedon
(1976). Recent systems theory has emphasized the merging of
COM and on-line access in a manner described in Section Three
of this report.

Library Applications

An initial, limited library interest in COM followed the
development of machine-readable bibliographic data bases during
the mid-1960's. Kozumplik and Lange (1967) reported the first
library-related application -- a catalog at the Lockheed
Technical Information Center. McGrath and Simon (1971) selected
COM as the output medium for the Louisiana Numerical Register,
a union catalog listing 1,100,000 holdings of twenty-one
libraries. The decision for COM was based on economy and speed

of production, two advantages of COM discussed in Section Three. Ungerleider (1973), Fischer (1973), and Bolef (1974) described the use of COM to replace line printer[*] output for in-process lists and other reports used by technical services staffs in public and academic libraries. Buckle and French (1971), Spencer (1973), and Buckle (1974) report the successful implementation of COM catalogs for use by patrons in British public and academic libraries. Aschenborn (1972), Stecher (1975), and Jacob (1975) reported similar applications in South African and Australian libraries. Reports of the patron use of COM in American libraries were presented by Roberts and Kennedy (1973) and Saffady (1974).

Spaulding and Fair (1975) noted the growing importance of COM in a review of library micrographics activity during the year 1974. The number of library COM applications has increased dramatically since that time. The currently intense library interest in COM has been stimulated by several important developments, including the growing availability of library holdings data in machine-readable form made possible by the Library of Congress' MARC program, combined with increased awareness of the high cost of maintaining conventional book and card-form catalogs. In the Baltimore County and Fairfax County (Virginia) public library systems, for example, COM catalogs and display equipment have proven to be a cost-effective replacement for printed book catalogs. One of the most important factors in the increased availability of machine-readable data for COM recording is the wide-spread use of the Ohio College Library Center system and the consequent availability of individual library holdings data on OCLC archival tapes. Autographics, Science Press, Brodart, Blackwell/North America and several other organizations have developed the software required to convert OCLC tapes to COM catalogs. In an application described by Meyer and Knapp (1975), for example, the University of Texas at Dallas provides Blackwell/North America with a bi-weekly OCLC tape containing holdings data to be recorded on a COM microfiche catalog.

The range of machine-readable input acceptable to companies offering such services is not limited to OCLC tapes. Most of them support COM catalog production with a wide range of data base maintenance and bibliographic services. The Brodart Collection Access System, for example, is designed to assist libraries in the creation and maintenance of a bibliographic data base of MARC-compatible records. Using an OCR typing element, the library prepares short entry records for items to be included in its data base. Brodart, using the information keyed by the library, searches its cumulative MARC data base to retrieve full catalog records. Four to six times per year, the data base is used to print cumulative COM catalogs in a format selected by the library. A list of vendors known to offer such services is provided in an appendix to this report.

While current library interest in COM has emphasized
catalog production, several larger libraries have selected
COM as the output medium for other types of computer-generated
reports. The New York Public Library, for example, has a
COM-produced in-process list that is used by technical services
staff. The Michigan State University Library has lists of
items in circulation printed on COM fiche. The New York State
Library has a serials KWIC index generated via COM.

COM for Micropublishing*

Library interest in COM has been further stimulated by
its increasingly successful use as a medium for the publication
of other bibliographic products and reference works. The
Library of Congress Cataloging Distribution Service now offers
Library of Congress Subject Headings, Eighth Edition on
forty-five 24X COM-generated microfiche or 4,508 frames of
16mm reel microfilm. The LCSH in microform which developed
out of a successful pilot project to test the acceptance and
utility of microform bibliographic products in technical service
applications, is distributed in advance of the printed version
and provides an excellent example of the speed advantages COM
enjoys over other recording media designed for computer output.
These advantages are discussed in Section Three of this report.
The Library of Congress also offers the Register of Locations
on COM-generated fiche or film. The first microform edition
contains location reports for approximately 1.75 million titles

through 1975. For this product, the economy of COM production
will permit subsequent issues to be continuously cumulative.
Because of the rapid production capability of COM and the
importance of the Register in inter-library loan, the Library
of Congress is attempting to determine the optimum frequency
of publication and the extent to which the COM version could
supplant the printed edition.

Some recently introduced original micropublications[*]
are created by COM from machine-readable bibliographic data
bases. The American Studies Bibliography, produced by the
Institute of United States Studies at the University of London,
is an example of the use of COM for the production of an economical
subject bibliography. Most COM-generated micropublications,
however, are MARC-derivative products designed to provide more
current bibliographic verification and cataloging data than
can be obtained through the National Union Catalog or other
printed sources. Examples of publications of this type include
Books in English, an ultrafiche micropublication produced by
the British Library from combined LC and UK MARC data bases;
MARCFICHE, a COM-generated bibliographic data base derived
from MARC tapes; the Cataloging-In-Publication data included
in the 3M Micrographic Catalog Retrieval System; and CARDSET,
a product of Information Design intended for the production of
catalog card sets, via Xerox Microprinter, from COM-generated
16mm roll microfilm.

Following the lead of national bibliography, a number of
trade bibliographies are issued as original COM micropublications.
Ingram's, the Nashville-based book seller, offers its customers
a weekly microfiche catalog and reader for a nominal charge.
The B/NA Title Index is a 1.2 million entry alphabetical
listing designed to facilitate bibliographic verification and
order preparation for Blackwell/North America customers.
Brodart's Book Information System is a million item 16mm COM-
generated data base reflecting virtually every title available
for sale through normal trade channels.

Among indexing and abstracting publications, Biofiche V
is a COM-generated cumulation of Biological Abstracts, 1970-74
which includes a completely re-processed annual index section.
For users of the DIALOG Information Retrieval Service, Lockheed
Information Systems offers the DIALIST, a COM-generated microfiche
listing of subject terms and their frequencies of occurrence
in various DIALOG data bases. DIALIST is designed to assist
in the determination of the utility of data base search
strategies prior to an actual on-line search and provides
an excellent example of an information system that combines
COM and on-line access for improved cost-effectiveness.

Several reference works have been produced by COM from
machine-readable data. Examples include the Import/Export
Microtables, published by Microeditions Hachette; S.C. Jacobson
et al, A Concordance to Joseph Conrad's Heart of Darkness

(Carbondale: Southern Illinois University Press, 1972); and

Aldo S. Bernardo, <u>A Concordance to the Familiari of S. Francisco</u>

<u>Petrarca</u> (Albany: State University of New York Press, 1977).

SECTION TWO

COM HARDWARE AND SOFTWARE

Non-Technical Summary

The purpose of this summary is to provide library
administrators and other non-technical personnel with a brief
overview to COM recording technology and to the basic
characteristics of currently available COM recorders and
data preparation techniques. The summary is followed by
a detailed discussion of COM hardware and software that is
intended primarily for library systems analysts and other
technical specialists.

The COM Recorder

A Computer-Output Microfilmer, or COM recorder, is both
a computer peripheral device[*] and a high-speed microfilmer.
As a computer peripheral, a COM recorder can operate on-line[*]
or off-line[*]. On-line COM recorders are connected to a computer
by wires and operate under its direct control, just as paper
printers do. The off-line COM recorder is a stand-alone device
that reads digital data from an appropriately formatted magnetic
tape[*]. The tape, resulting from the execution of a computer
program, must be brought to the COM recorder and mounted on
an integral or attached tape drive. Off-line COM recorders
can be located at some distance from the computer on which

the input tape is prepared and are widely used by service bureaus and other vendors offering COM services to libraries.

Regardless of mode of operation, logical circuits within the COM recorder translate digital input into a combination of information to be recorded and machine instructions. The machine instructions indicate which data is to be recorded and in what size and position. The data is then recorded on microfilm in one of four ways: 1) by photographing a cathode-ray-tube (CRT) display; 2) by exposing microfilm to a light-emitting-diode (LED) display; 3) by an electron beam; or 4) by a laser beam. The four recording methods differ in speed, capabilities, and recording media utilized. Cathode-ray-tube* photography remains the most prevalent COM recording technology. It is fast and versatile. Depending on the method of character generation, the lower case alphabet, foreign characters, and other special symbols required in library applications can be recorded. CRT-type COM recorders employ silver-halide microfilm which is capable of archival quality processing for long-term preservation. LED recording, now used by only one COM manufacturer, is relatively slow and lacks the typographic versatility and image quality required in many library applications. As in CRT recording, LED-type recorders employ silver-halide microfilm. Electron beam and laser beam COM recorders can utilize unconventional, dry-processed microfilm and are, consequently, well-suited to placement in computer centers where the external plumbing required to process silver-halide microfilm may not be available. While dry-processed microfilms are convenient, their relative useful life and permanence has not been established.

17

All four COM recording technologies permit the super-imposition of a transparent piece of glass or film bearing the image of a business form on the data as it is recorded, thereby emulating report production on pre-printed form stock.

Data Preparation

As noted above, off-line COM recorders read digital data from an appropriately-formatted magnetic tape. Librarians considering the implementation of one or more COM applications must determine which tape sizes, densities, and coding formats are acceptable to the recorder to be used. In addition, off-line COM recorders require that data and embedded machine commands be presented on tape in a prescribed format. Preparation of the input tape is the library's responsibility and requires special software.[*] For most libraries, the simplest way to implement a COM application is to select a service bureau[*] equipped with a minicomputer-controlled[*] COM recorder. The library then need only create magnetic tape containing data suitable for output on a line printer. The minicomputer attached to the COM recorder contains software necessary to automatically restructure the data for COM output. Additional host computer time and programmer involvement are not required. Where minicomputer-controlled COM recorders are unavailable, the library must either modify its application programs to incorporate special formatting subroutines[*] or utilize a

18

translator program[*] to create a COM input tape from data
intended for output on a line printer. While formatting
subroutines and translator programs can usually be obtained
from COM manufacturers without charge, some additional computer
time and programmer involvement are required.

On-line COM recorders are designed to emulate conventional
line printers and require no special input preparation in the
conversion of paper reports to unindexed roll microfilm. To
produce microfiche or indexed roll microfilm, however, the
applications programs must be modified to include formatting
subroutines.

The COM Recorder

A Computer-Output-Microfilmer, or COM recorder, is both
a computer peripheral device and a high-speed microfilmer.
As a computer peripheral a COM recorder can operate on-line
or off-line. Four micro-recording technologies are in current
use.

Modes of Operation

On-line COM recorders -- such as the Memorex 1603, Cal Comp
2130/2131, and DatagraphiX 4520 -- are connected to a computer
and operate under its direct control (fig. 1). Digital data
to be recorded on microfilm is received directly from the
computer. All currently-available on-line COM recorders are
designed for operation with IBM System 360/370 computers.

19

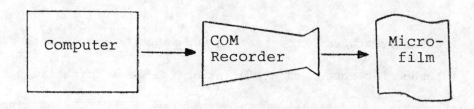

On-Line Recording

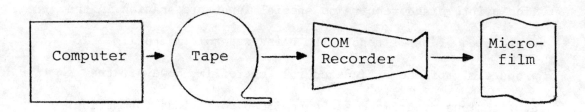

Off-Line Recording

Fig. 1

Modes of COM Recorder Operation

Presumably, on-line COM recorders will also operate with the new IBM-compatible mainframes, such as the Amdahl 470 or the Itel AS/5. Interface to the central processor is through a selector or multiplexor channel. Generally, the on-line recorder requires the equivalent of a System 360, model 25 and above, or any System 370. The computer interacts with the on-line COM recorder as it does with the equivalent of an IBM 1403 line printer.

Most COM recorders, however, are operated off-line. The off-line COM recorder is a stand-alone device that reads digital data from an appropriately-formatted magnetic tape. The tape, resulting from the execution of a computer program, must be brought to the COM recorder and mounted on an internal or attached tape drive (fig. 2). The tape may be formatted on any one of a wide range of general-purpose computers, using one of several software techniques described later in this section. Alternatively, the off-line COM recorder may incorporate a programmable minicomputer designed to create appropriately-formatted and indexed microforms from conventional printer tapes.

The cost of the required magnetic tape drive makes the off-line COM recorder substantially more expensive than on-line models. Off-line recorders are more versatile, however. Most available units will accept input tapes prepared on a wide range of general-purpose computers. On-line recorders, as

Mounting of Tape

Insertion of Job Card

Insertion of Form Slide

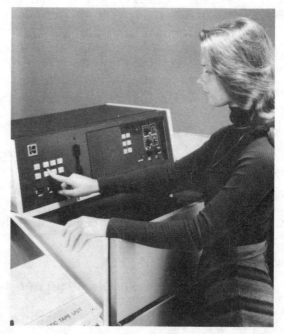

Start-Up

<u>Figure 2</u>
Operation of an Off-Line COM Recorder
(Courtesy: Eastman Kodak)

already noted, are limited to the IBM System 360/370 environment.
Because the off-line COM recorder is not connected to a computer,
availability and productivity need not be limited by computer
downtime. In cases of COM recorder malfunction, jobs can be
re-run without additional computer involvement and, as noted
in Section Three, in much less time than with a line printer.
Off-line COM recorders may be located at some distance from
the computer on which the input tape is prepared and are widely
used by microfilm service bureaus and other vendors offering
COM services to libraries. Additional points of comparison
are discussed by Bolnick (1971).

Recording Methods

Regardless of mode of operation, logical circuits within
the COM recorder translate digital input into a combination
of information to be recorded and machine instructions. The
machine instructions indicate which data is to be recorded
and in what size and position. The data is then recorded on
microfilm in one of four ways: 1) by photographing a cathode-
ray-tube display; 2) by exposing microfilm to a light-emitting
diode display; 3) by an electron beam; or 4) by a laser beam.

Cathode-ray-tube (CRT photography) the oldest and most
prevalent COM recording technology, is used in computer-output-
microfilmers sold by Bell and Howell, Cal Comp, DatagraphiX,
Information International, Kodak, Quantor, 3M, and others.

Data from magnetic tape, or, in the case of on-line COM recorders, from the computer itself, is typically displayed as a page of information on the screen of a CRT located inside the COM recorder. The CRT display is then photographed by a high-speed microfilm camera, the film advanced, the display erased, a new page displayed, and the process repeated (fig. 3). Recording speeds range from two to five pages per second, depending on the recorder and the method of input presentation.

The method of character generation on the CRT screen varies with the manufacturer. DatagraphiX COM recorders use the Charactron^{TM} shaped beam tube which forms individual characters by directing a stream of electrons through appropriate positions on a small template located in the neck of the CRT (fig. 4). The Charactron tube, developed by the Convair division of General Dynamics during the 1950's, has been used in DatagraphiX COM recorders since that time. The new DatagraphiX 4500 Series COM recorders feature an improved Charactron tube that is up to twelve times brighter than earlier models, thus producing an improved image.

COM recorders sold by Cal Comp, Information International, Kodak and 3M use electron beam strokes to define characters on the CRT screen. Bell and Howell and Quantor recorders define individual characters from light points in a dot matrix* on the CRT screen. For library applications, the method of character generation in CRT-type COM recorders is of

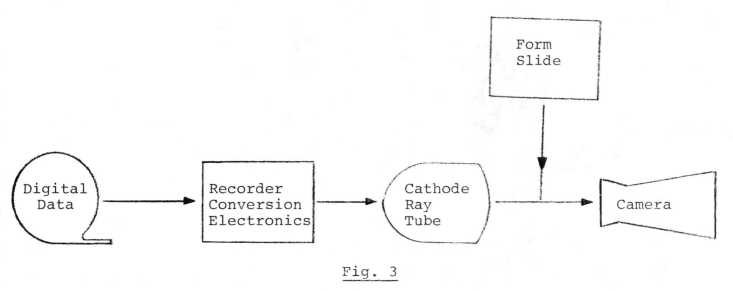

Fig. 3

COM Recording by CRT Photography

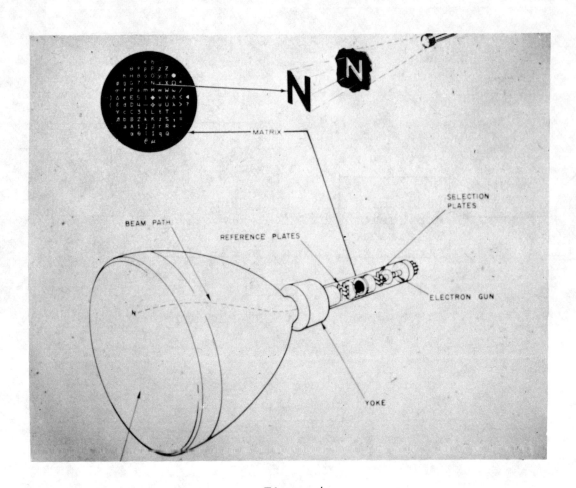

Figure 4
Charactron Shaped Beam Tube Used in DatagraphiX COM Recorders
(Courtesy: DatagraphiX, Inc.)

particular importance because of its relationship to image
quality and character set expansion. This relationship is
discussed in the next section of this report.

Regardless of the method of character generation, the
recording medium in CRT photography is typically a blue-sensitive,
low-contrast, black-and-white silver-halide microfilm designed
for rapid processing. The Information International FR-80 is
currently the only COM recorder capable of producing full-color
microimages. In most cases, the exposed silver-halide microfilm
is removed from the recorder and taken to a separate processor.
The Quantor 105 and 115 and the DatagraphiX Auto COM are
integrated COM recorder/processors that will expose, develop,
and deliver cut, dry microfiche in one continuous operation.
Throughput speed is about one 42:1 microfiche per minute.
Chemicals are furnished in pre-mixed containers for ease of
replenishment. The development of this COM product group is
discussed by Titus (1972). These integrated recorder/processors
are well-suited to computer room installations where operating
personnel lack microphotographic experience and the external
plumbing required by conventional film processors is unavailable.

Light-emitting-diode (LED) recording attracted much attention
during the 1960's but is currently used only by the Memorex
1603 COM printer. As described by Herbert (1971), the Memorex
1603 uses a bank of light-emitting-diodes to create and record
a line of up to 132 characters. Each character is formed from

a five by seven matrix of very fine light-conducting glass rods. These rods are selectively illuminated to shape the desired characters. The completed line is then exposed to a special silver-halide microfilm sensitive to infrared energy. Following exposure, the film is advanced, a new line formed, and the process repeated. Recording speed is approximately 10,000 lines per minute or two to three pages per second. Exposed microfilm is processed and duplicated in a conventional manner.

LED recording is distinguished by reliability, simplicity, and relatively low cost. At less than $50,000, the price of a Memorex 1603 is half that of many other COM recorders and compares favorably with the price of the fastest line printers. The unit offers little flexibility, however. It operates exclusively on-line, producing 16mm microfilm in the cine[*] mode only. This, combined with the inability to produce microfiche, restricts the utility of LED recording in many library applications. While the factory-sealed display section requires very little maintenance, the character set is limited and cannot be expanded.

In both CRT photography and LED recording, as noted by Norcross and Sampath (1973), the total amount of light at the film plane is relatively low. The recording medium is consequently restricted to silver-halide photographic materials with the attendant inconvenience of wet chemical processing. Micro-recording onto vesicular, diazo, or other unconventional, dry-processed photographic materials requires an order of magnitude increase in CRT or LED energy output. At the present time, only one CRT-type COM recorder, the 3M 715, permits recording onto non-conventional photographic media. The 3M 715, introduced in October, 1977, employs a bright orange CRT display to expose microimages on 3M Brand dry silver film, described more fully below. Other available COM recorders employ alternative recording technologies to expose dry silver film. Two such technologies are currently used in the United States: laser beam recording and electron beam recording.

The potential of lasers in micro-recording systems was first described in detail by Meyers (1971). In laser-beam COM recording, a low-power helium-neon laser is used to activate and expose points in a dot matrix pattern on film (fig. 5). Laser beams can be directed with great precision and turned on and off at very high speeds. When the laser scans a matrix on film, the beam exposes only those points necessary to shape individual characters. Mirrors are used to move the laser from line to line across pages. Effective recording speeds approximate 10,000 lines per minute or two to three pages per second. Unlike conventional light which consists of a mixture of wavelengths or colors, laser light is concentrated and,

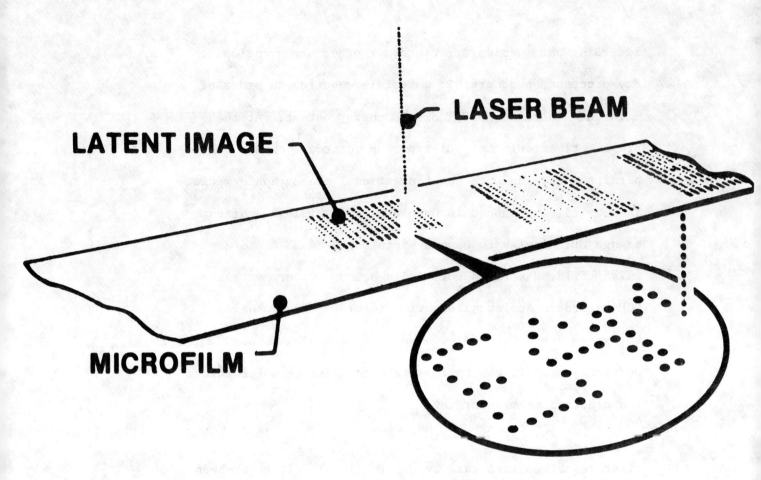

Figure 5
Laser Beam COM Recording
(Courtesy: 3M Company)

consequently, much more powerful. Like electron beams, lasers
can generate the energy required to expose unconventional
photographic media. The 3M Laser Beam Recorder (LBR), for
example, uses 3M Brand dry silver film. Dry silver microfilm
is a light-sensitive recording medium that is developed by
the application of heat alone. Its general properties are
discussed by Shepard (1973). The dry silver processor can be
attached directly to the 3M EBR for continuous operation and
delivery of developed, immediately usable microimages. Because
the development of dry silver microfilm does not require
plumbing or chemicals, electron beam recording is well-suited
to the production of computer-output-microfilm in the computer
room itself. Dry silver microfilm is also the recording medium
utilized by the 3M 1050 Step-and-Repeat source document camera.
The Kodak Komstar Microimage Processor, a recently-introduced
laser-beam recorder, exposes Dacomatic DL film, a fine-grain
silver-halide microfilm with embedded chemicals for dry processing.

The 3M Electron Beam Recorder (EBR) reads digital data
from magnetic tape and deflects an electron beam that strokes
latent character images directly onto dry silver microfilm at
the rate of two to five pages per second. Operation of the EBR
is described by Firisen (1971). A similar system developed
by Image Graphics Incorporated for the Army Engineering Topographic
Laboratories is described by Grosso and Tarnowski (1976). In
both cases, the electron beam functions much like a pencil of
light, writing the individual characters on the film itself.

Libraries considering electron beam or laser-beam recording should be aware that, unlike silver-halide microfilm, the relative permanence of dry silver microfilm has not been determined. Dry silver films do remain sensitive to light and heat following initial exposure. Kurttila (1977) reports an analysis of dry silver films eight to ten years old which supports predictions of a twenty-five year or longer life expectancy. For those COM applications requiring archival quality for long-term preservation, a silver-halide duplicate must be made from the dry silver master.

Forms Recording

To emulate report production on pre-printed form stock, all COM recorders will merge dynamic digital data with a static format. This is normally accomplished with a form slide, a transparent piece of glass or film bearing the image of a business form with blank spaces for variable information to be filled in from the input data stream (fig. 6). The form slide image in superimposed on the data during recording, using a mirror. As noted by Pauer (1976), form slide artwork must be designed for optimum reproducibility at high reductions. Line placement accuracy is crucial to proper registration of the form image and data. In addition to the creation of custom form slides for special applications, Photographic Sciences Corporation and other companies offer a number of standard form slides of general utility. These standard form slides feature lines,

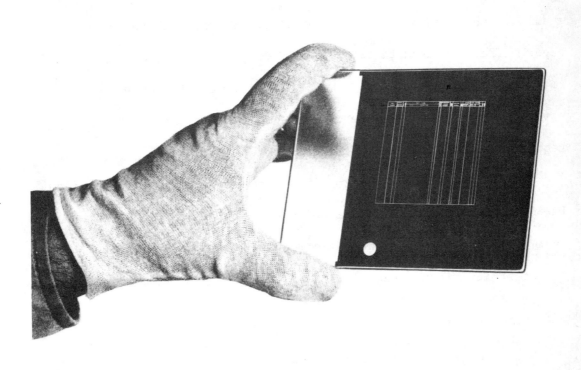

Figure 6
A COM Form Slide
(Courtesy: Photographic Sciences Corporation)

shading, and frame borders and are analagous to stock computer paper. They are used to establish frame limits and speed retrieval of columnar data. Some COM recorders will store several form slides and interchange them automatically, as required, within the same microform.

As an alternative to form slides, the Information International FR-80 COM recorder stores form definitions in memory and strokes them, with the data, on the CRT screen under program control. This technique is necessarily slower than the form slide approach.

Input Preparation Requirements

As noted in the preceding sub-section on modes of operation, off-line COM recorders read digital input from magnetic tape. Librarians considering the conversion of one or more reports to COM must determine which tape sizes, recording densities, and coding formats are acceptable to the recorder to be used. In addition, off-line COM recorders require that data and embedded machine commands be recorded on tape in prescribed formats. Input preparation for on-line COM recording is typically simpler but still requires attention.

Tapes Accepted

Most of the off-line COM recorders used by microfilm service bureaus incorporate a universal tape drive which will accept seven or nine track, NRZI or PE tapes at recording densities of 200, 556, 800, or 1600 bits per inch. As an option, the

Bell and Howell 3700 and 3800 COM recorders will accept tapes recorded at 6250 bits per inch. Less versatile units, often used by corporate or institutional data processing centers equipped with computers of a single manufacturer, will accept only specific tape sizes recorded at specific densities. COM recorder manufacturers generally offer a specific tape drive as standard equipment with a universal tape drive available as an extra cost option. A few newer models -- the 3M LBR, for example -- offer the universal tape drive as a standard component.

In terms of tape coding, all available off-line COM recorders will read EBCDIC* code, the internal system code of IBM 360/370 computers. Most off-line COM recorders will also read ASCII* code, used widely by non-IBM computers, and BCD* code, used by the IBM 1401, a second generation computer no longer manufactured but still in use. In some cases, EBCDIC is the COM system standard code with ASCII and BCD translators available only as factory-installed options. Again, newer models tend to be more versatile, incorporating several code translators that are switch-selectable by the operator at run-time. A few off-line COM recorders -- the Bell and Howell 3700, for example -- will accept tapes prepared by Honeywell, NCR, and other computers with special code structures.

Tape Preparation

As noted above, off-line COM recorders require a specially-formatted magnetic tape containing both the data to be recorded on microfilm and embedded machine commands. These machine

commands instruct the COM recorder to begin a new line, frame,

or fiche; change type font, size, or intensity; indent to

present information in columns; and so on. Magnetic tapes

containing data to be recorded on microfiche must also include

instructions for the content and placement of eye-legible titling

and for the derivation of index information from the data

itself. Machine commands are typically unique to each COM

recorder. The repertoire of interpretable commands varies

with the capabilities of the recorder.

The formatting of COM tapes requires special software

capable of appending special control characters to print-data

generated by the user's application program. COM software is

an important, but neglected, subject last reviewed by Peoples

(1972). Three software alternatives are currently available:

1) modification of application programs to call special

formatting subroutines; 2) the use of translator programs

to reformat line printer records for COM; and 3) reliance on

a minicomputer-controlled COM recorder with resident reformatting

software. The three alternatives differ significantly in the

relative involvement of programmer time, the host computer,

and the COM recorder itself.

The Subroutine Method

COM formatting subroutines consist of specially-prepared

machine instructions which, when linked to the library's

application program, will intercept normal print records and restructure them as output suitable for COM recording. With IBM computers operating under DOS, for example, programs which write to the printer automatically interface with PRMOD (PRinter MODule), an IBM-supplied system subroutine designed to convert the logical print-format records of the application program to the physical print-format records required by a line printer (fig. 7). COM formatting subroutines replace PRMOD, producing records to be written onto a magnetic tape which is, in turn, taken to the COM recorder (fig. 8). Implementation is similar in other operating system environments.

All COM recorder manufacturers make one or more pre-written and pre-tested software packages available to customers, usually without charge. These software packages are typically written in assembler language for IBM System 360/370 computers and in ANSI COBOL for computers of other manufacturers. Most vendor-supplied subroutines can be called from application programs written in COBOL, FORTRAN, PL/1, or assembler language and are usually called with each line of print-data. Some COM manufacturers -- Kodak and 3M, for example -- offer extensive subroutine libraries. Alternatively, users may write their own subroutines -- as Boeing did for a library catalog application described by Rogers and Vogt (1973) -- or obtain them from service bureaus or other third parties. U.S. Datacorp, the world's largest COM service bureau, maintains a software library of more than 400 programs. The COMDEX package, offered by

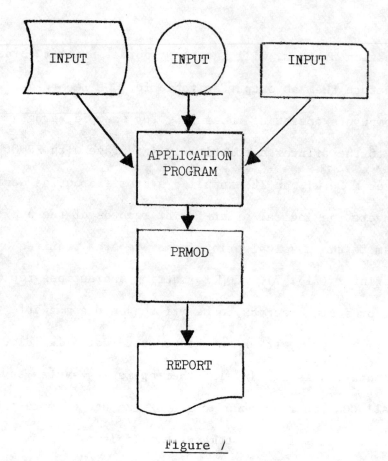

Figure /

Formatting of Line Printer Records Under DOS

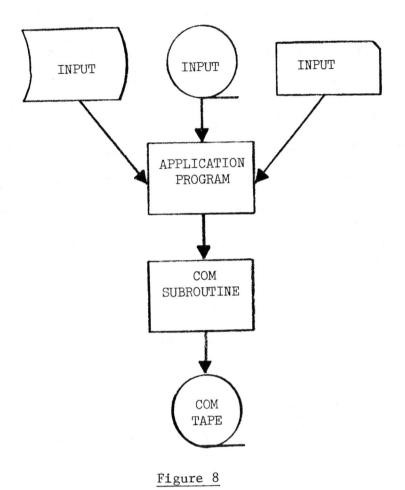

Figure 8

The Subroutine Method of COM Input Preparation

Wright Data Systems, is a COM indexing program that can be used to create titled indexed microfiche in a variety of formats and reductions on any recorder with microfiche output capability.

The subroutine method is generally flexible and efficient. Because it creates a formatted COM tape in a single computer run, the subroutine method should be seriously considered for library programs that are executed frequently. While the resulting savings in host computer charges can prove significant when compared to the other formatting methods described later in this section, such savings must be weighed against the cost of required programmer involvement. The best subroutine packages -- Quantor's AME (Automatic Microfiche Editor), for example -- minimize required program modifications and simplify implementation while providing user-exits that allow the programmer to add locally-written code in order to satisfy special application requirements. Most COM record structures are designed, however, to conform to those of the IBM System 360/370. As a general rule, the subroutine method will prove easiest to implement in the IBM computer environment. The level of required programming effort will typically be greater with other computers.

Two other potential limitations of the subroutine method should be noted: there is a minimum core requirement that varies with the package, and the host computer must support the programming language in which the subroutines are written.

In the general-purpose computer environment, these are rarely limitations, but some of the minicomputers that are increasingly used by libraries have small amounts of main memory and do not support an ANSI COBOL compiler.

Print-Tape Translation

In most general-purpose computer environments, the output resulting from execution of an application program is written onto a tape, or occasionally a disk, from which it is later printed. This technique, called spooling, is designed to minimize inefficiencies resulting from the speed differential between the central processing unit and the output devices, notably the line printer. The file of print-records created in this way is variously called a spool-tape, a print-tape, or a print-file. COM print-tape translation packages read and reconstruct these records, producing a COM tape with appropriate embedded machine commands (fig. 9). Typically, the user provides titling, indexing, and other application parameters. Most COM manufacturers provide print-tape translators for a wide range of general purpose computers. Some translator packages, like Quantor's FAME (Formatting Automatic Microfiche Editor), permit optional printing of paper reports from COM tapes or selective copying of specified fiche records from one tape to another.

Unlike the subroutine method, the library using print-tape translation to convert applications from paper to COM will not

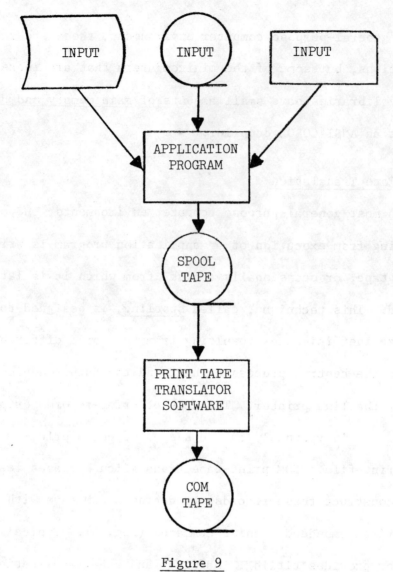

Figure 9

The Print Tape Translation Method

generally require the services of a programmer. Separate computer runs are necessary, however, to first produce, then translate, the print-tape. For library programs executed frequently, host computer charges may increase significantly.

Bell and Howell's COMDATA report-generator software package is an example of an interesting alternative to conventional print-tape translation. COMDATA significantly reduces the software effort necessary for conversion to COM by creating fully-titled, indexed, and formatted microfiche directly from raw data files without an application program. The user provides application parameters on cards at run time. The basic package, currently available only for the IBM System 360/370, operates in 50K of core under DOS. The OS/360 core requirement is dynamic. In addition to report-generation, the COMDATA package will also function as a conventional print-tape translator.

Minicomputer-controlled COM Recorders

An increasing number of COM recorders incorporate minicomputers with software to reformat print-tapes prepared on a wide range of general-purpose computers, thereby freeing the user's host computer of the responsibility for print-tape translation. The minicomputer used varies with the COM manufacturer. The Bell and Howell 3800, for example, uses a DEC PDP-11/04 capable of controlling up to four COM recorders. The DatagraphiX 4550 and 4560 employ a Lockheed SUE. The Quantor 115 incorporates an

NCR 606. Reformatting software, with the user's application parameters, are typically stored on tape cartridges, cassettes, or diskettes. A Teletype ASR-33 or equivalent terminal permits communication between system and operator.

Minicomputer software eliminates the need for an intermediate COM tape. Minicomputer-controlled COM recorders produce microform output directly from a user-supplied print-tape. By using a service bureau equipped with a minicomputer-controlled COM recorder, a library can quickly and easily convert any printer-oriented output to COM. This input preparation alternative is especially attractive to libraries without access to host computer time for print-tape formatting. In an application described by Saffady (1974), the Wayne State University Libraries converted a computer-generated serials holdings list from paper output to 16mm microfilm cassettes, utilizing a COM service bureau equipped with a minicomputer-controlled Gould Beta COM 700L (now the 3M Beta COM 700H). Following each execution of the holdings list updating program, the library gives the service bureau a print-tape containing records suitable for an IBM 1403 line printer. A PDP-8/E minicomputer attached to the Beta COM performs the necessary print-tape translation for COM output.

In addition to tape translation, most minicomputer software will generate printed reports of the number of lines, frames, or fiche produced by the recorder, as well as other useful job statistics. In some cases, the minicomputer can be programmed to perform additional manipulation of the input data prior to recording on microfilm.

Data Preparation for On-Line Recording

On-line COM recorders, as already noted, will accept
digital input from IBM System 360/370 computers or IBM-compatible
mainframes. The production of printer page-images on unindexed
16mm roll microfilm usually requires no modification of application
programs. The Memorex 1603, for example, will respond to all
IBM 1403 and 1443 print commands.

To produce microfiche or indexed roll microfilm, application
programs must be modified to call formatting subroutines. These
subroutines, which are available from COM recorder manufacturers,
are virtually identical with those used to prepare COM tapes
for off-line recording. Because the elimination of spooling
and intermediate print-files is one of the justifications for
on-line COM recording, print-tape translation is not an applicable
software alternative.

Emulation Software

Emulation software permits a COM recorder to accept
unconverted input tapes prepared for other COM recorders.
The availability of emulation software enables libraries to
convert their COM applications to alternative hardware,
without reprogramming, in the event of recorder malfunction
or unsatisfactory service bureau response. Because of its
historical dominance of the COM market, emulation software

is most widely available for DatagraphiX recorders. The Bell and Howell 3700, Quantor 105, and several other COM recorders will accept DatagraphiX-formatted tapes. The 3M Beta COM recorders will accept input tapes prepared for DatagraphiX recorders, the 3M EBR, 3M LBR, Kodak KOM-80 and KOM-90, and the now defunct Rand COM. The Information International FR-80 will emulate a wide range of COM units, including DatagraphiX and Cal Comp recorders.

Output Capabilities

COM recorders are available for the production of both roll and flat microforms in a variety of formats and reductions. Depending on the recorder, data recorded on film or fiche may be alphanumeric, graphic, or both.

Microforms Produced

Most available COM recorders will produce both 16mm roll microfilm and standard 105 by 148mm (approximately four by six inch) microfiche. Some COM recorders introduced prior to 1970 -- the Memorex 1603 and 3M EBR, for example -- will produce only 16mm roll microfilm, for use on reels, in cartridges and cassettes, or in jackets. Several newer COM recorders, reflecting changes in the popularity of the various microforms, will produce only microfiche. In some newer COM recorders -- the DatagraphiX 4500 Series, for example -- the microfiche camera is standard and the ability to produce 16mm microfilm is

available only as an extra cost option. This represents a
significant change from earlier COM recorders, notably the
DatagraphiX 4360 and 4440, which offered 16mm microfilm as
standard output and microfiche as an extra-cost option.

The use of 35mm microfilm, the most popular microform
for library source document applications, is generally limited
to COM-generated graphics, engineering drawings, and multi-page
alphanumeric records intended for insertion in aperture cards.
A significant exception is Books in English, the British
library micropublication which is first recorded via COM on
35mm roll microfilm, then further reduced by NCR to create
ultrafiche masters. This innovative application is described
by Ardern (1971) and Linford (1972).

A few COM recorders, including the Kodak KOM-80 and
DatagraphiX 4540, will produce the tab-size microfiche
(3 1/4 by 7 3/8 inches) used by IBM for its technical publications.

Effective Reduction Ratios and Internal Formats

Microforms, by definition, present information in reduced
size. In source document applications, reduction is a measure
of the number of times a given linear dimension of a document
is reduced through microphotography. This measure is expressed
as 14:1, 24:1, 42:1, and so on, where the reduced linear
dimension of 1/14, 1/24, or 1/42 the length of its full-size
counterpart. Because actual documents are not involved in COM
recording, COM reduction ratios are termed effective reduction ratios.

The effective reduction ratio is a statement of the number of times a given linear dimension of an imaginary document would have to be reduced to equal the size of the corresponding linear dimension of a COM microimage. In most cases, the imaginary document is an eleven by fourteen inch computer printout page. In CRT-type COM recorders, the display that is microfilmed is typically smaller than the imaginary document it represents. In the Cal Comp 2100 Series COM recorders, for example, the CRT display measures 2.200 by 1.833 inches -- a 6:1 reduction of computer print out size.

The most widely-used effective reduction ratios for 16mm roll microfilm and microfiche are 24:1, 42:1, and 48:1. On 16mm roll microfilm, a COM recorder such as the 3M EBR will record the equivalent of one computer printout page per frame at 24:1, two computer printout pages per frame at 42:1, or four computer printout pages per frame at 48:1. Depending on the effective reduction, the total capacity of a one hundred foot roll ranges from about 2,000 to about 8,000 microimages. With the exception of the Memorex 1603, COM recorders will orient 16mm microimages in comic as well as cine mode (fig. 10). In the comic mode, lines of text run parallel to the edges of the microfilm. In the cine mode, lines of text run perpendicular to the edges of the microfilm.

The three most popular COM microfiche formats described by Avedon (1976), provide for sixty-three computer printout

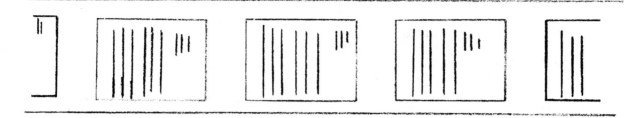

Cine Mode
(Lines of Text Perpendicular to Edges of Film)

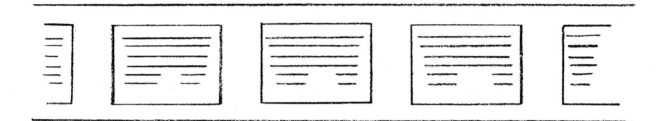

Comic Mode
(Lines of Text Parallel to Edges of Film)

Fig. 10

Placement of 16mm COM Images

pages in seven rows and nine columns at 24:1 effective reduction
ratio (fig. 11); 208 computer printout pages in thirteen rows
and sixteen columns at 42:1 (fig. 12); and 270 computer printout
pages in fifteen rows and eighteen columns at 48:1 (fig. 13).
The historical development of these particular reductions and
formats is discussed by Bernstein (1972).

As a linear measure, reduction does not state the total reduction
in document area achieved through microphotography. The microimage of a document or CRT display reduced 24:1, for example,
actually occupies 1/576 the area of the original. When silver
halide photographic materials are utilized to make large area
reductions, fewer silver halide grains are available in any
given area of film to define the shape of individual characters
in the original document. In conventional microphotography,
the variable quality of newspapers, monographs, and similar
library source documents has traditionally argued for the use
of 35mm microfilm and the lowest possible reduction ratios
to ensure legibility through several generations of microform
duplicates.[1] Within the COM recorder, however, careful control

---

[1] Forbes and Bagg (1966), in a National Bureau of Standards
study of the photometric characteristics of bound serials and
monographs in the National Library of Medicine, recommended a
maximum reduction of 12X to insure preservation of legibility
throughout the archival collection. Hawken (1968), following
an extensive study of the typographic characteristics of printed
text, suggested a maximum reduction of 12.7X to insure legibility
and duplicability in the micro-reproduction of the widest range
of library materials. Even with the improved quality of today's
source documents, the current NMA standard for microfiche made
from source documents recommends a 24X reduction for letter-size
documents.

Type 3   24X   11 x 14 Page Size   63 Frames

ANSI Standard PH5.18 (NMA MS2), ISO Draft International Standard DIS 5126

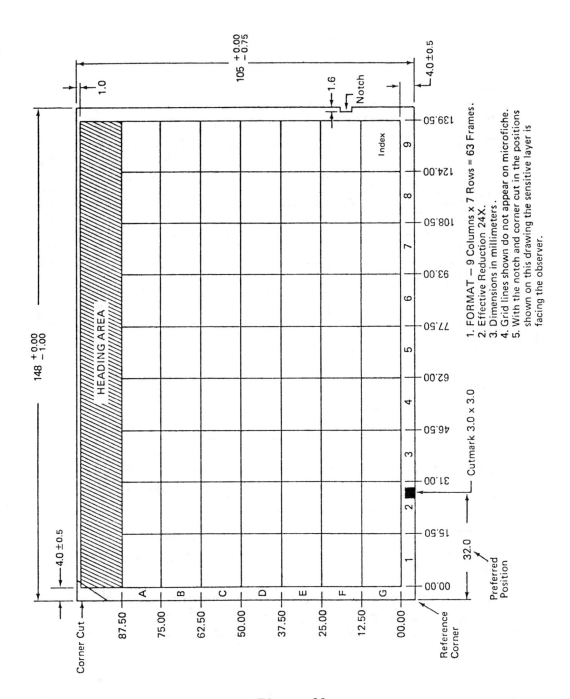

Figure 11
NMA Type 3, 24X COM Microfiche Format
(Courtesy: National Micrographics Association)

51

Appendix to ANSI Standard PH5.18 (NMA MS2)

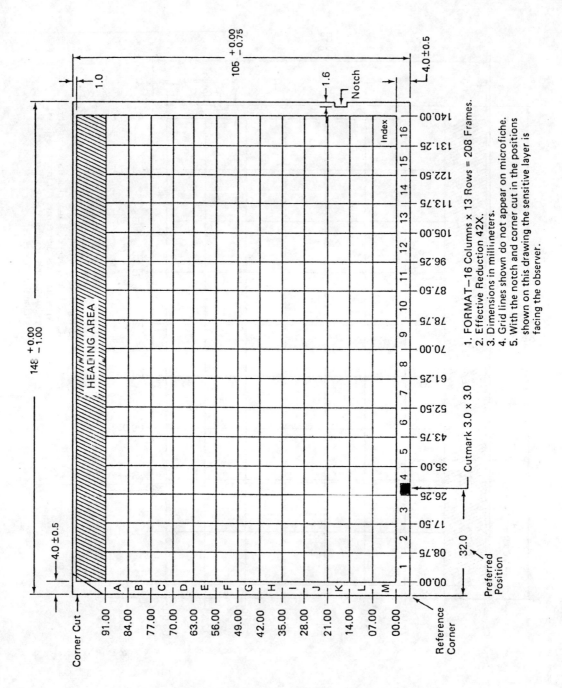

Figure 12
NMA Type 5, 42X COM Microfiche Format
(Courtesy: National Micrographics Association)

Type 7   48X   11 x 14 Page Size   270 Frames

Appendix to ANSI Standard PH5.18 (NMA MS2), ISO Draft International Standard DIS 5126, Military Standard MIL-F-80242

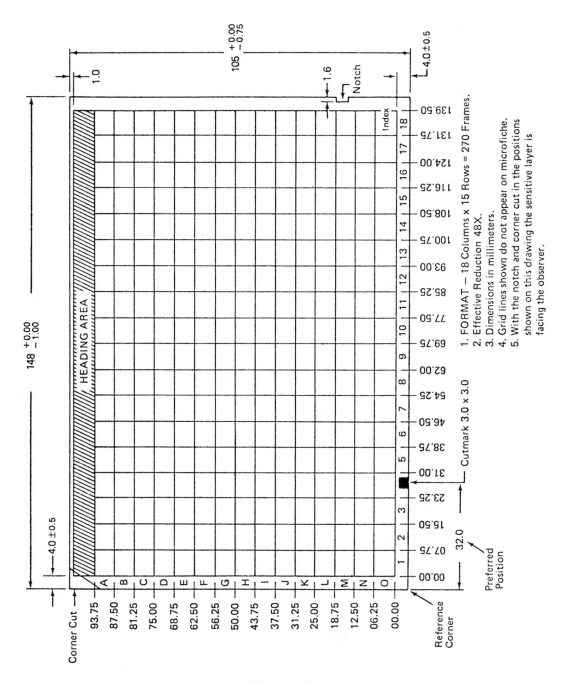

Figure 13
NMA Type 7, 48X COM Microfiche Format
(Courtesy: National Micrographics Association)

of character font, and image density permits the use of reduction ratios well in excess of those considered suitable for source document microphotography. The popularity of higher reduction ratios is indicated by the fact that the DatagraphiX Auto COM, one of the newest COM recorders, will produce only 42:1 or 48:1 microimages. 24:1, the source document standard, is not available. While 48:1 is the maximum effective reduction for most currently available COM recorders, Heacock (1975) contends that improvements in microfilm emulsions will eventually permit high-quality, single-step reductions in excess of 100:1. U.S. Datacorp, the world's largest COM service bureau, has customized recorders capable of producing high-quality microfiche with 690 images reduced 72:1, and has experimented with 96:1 reduction ratios. The 3M Beta COM 800, a CRT-type recorder, can reduce its display size by fifty percent for microfilming with a 48:1 lens, thereby achieving an effective reduction of 96:1. The Kodak Komstar recorders can be equipped with an optional feature that permits effective reductions of 72:1 and 96:1 through the use of a reduced-size character matrix.

Within a COM microfiche, pagination typically proceeds vertically -- down columns and across rows. Most COM recorders will also paginate horizontally, the standard for source documents. Some recorders will paginate down one column and up the next, a convenient, but little-used, format that

minimizes microfiche carrier movements during continuous

reading and in searches involving serial examination of

microimages.

Alphanumeric vs Graphic Recording

As noted in a preceding section of this report, COM

recorders have historically served two broad application

areas: alphanumeric* (business) and graphic* (scientific).

As the name implies, alphanumeric COM units will record only

alphabetic characters, numeric digits, punctuation marks,

and other symbols commonly used in textual documents.

Graphic COM recorders have full alphanumeric capability and

can also construct complex charts, graphs, plots, network

diagrams, and circuit drawings. Lamar and Stratton (1974)

describe the use of a DatagraphiX 4060 graphics COM recorder

to produce weather maps that represent contour intervals of

such variables as cloudiness, temperature, and precipitation

as shades of grey. In such scientific and technical applications,

graphic COM recorders offer a ten to twenty-fold improvement

in work throughput when compared to mechanical pen plotters

and permit merging of text and illustrative material in the

same microimage. The increasing use of COM for scientific

graphics is analyzed in an excellent article by Hirschsohn

(1977).

Although the earliest COM recorders had graphics capability, the majority of currently available units are exclusively alphanumeric. Being more complex, graphic COM recorders are necessarily more expensive than alphanumeric units. While prices for off-line alphanumeric COM recorders begin at $50,000, graphic recorders are priced in the $100,000 to $250,000 range, depending on capabilities. Regardless of cost, scientific graphics recording is of little significance to most libraries. Of potentially great importance, however, are the small number of essentially alphanumeric COM recorders with limited business graphics capability. The 3M Beta COM 700H, for example, will construct line charts, bar charts, pie charts, labelled axes, histograms, and other graphic presentations useful in management summary reports. The applications of COM business graphics are discussed by Doran (1971), Wells (1972), and Horst (1974).

COM Duplication

Master COM microforms can be duplicated on several film stocks, the choice depending on desired microimage polarity and the need for archival quality. Equipment is available for the duplication of COM microforms in both a production and an office-type environment.

Duplicating Film Stocks

Microform duplication is the production of single or multiple microform copies from a master microform. The master microform may be an original camera microform, created by source document microphotography or computer-output-microfilming, or a duplicate one or more generations removed from the camera original. Unlike original COM recording, which is an optical process, duplicate COM microforms are made by contact printing onto silver-halide, diazo, or vesicular film stock. The vesicular and diazo processes are the most widely used in COM duplication.

Vesicular microforms have a light sensitive layer made up of diazonium salts in a thermo plastic coating which is applied to a polyester base. Exposure to ultraviolet light transmitted through the clear areas of a master microform causes the diazonium salts to decompose and create microscopic pressure pockets of trapped nitrogen gas that form a latent image. Development is accomplished by the rapid application of heat which softens the thermo plastic briefly and allows the gas to form tiny bubbles (vesicles) which create the visible image. The plastic re-hardens when heat is removed fixing the image. Subsequent applications of heat must be avoided. Vesicular technology is described in detail by McGregor (1975).

The vesicular process requires no chemicals and is convenient, fast, and odorless. Its main advantage in COM duplication, however, derives from the fact that vesicular microfilms reverse the polarity of the master microform.

When developed normally, camera original microforms produced by the four COM recording technologies described earlier in this section will be of positive polarity -- that is, alphanumeric characters and graphic representations appear dark on a light background. This is true of both silver halide and dry silver microfilms. Negative COM microforms are generally preferred for viewing and for use in reader/printers, which may themselves reverse polarity in making prints from displayed images. The vesicular process is the fastest, most convenient way to create negative COM duplicates from positive COM masters.

Although vesicular microimages are particularly resistant to rough handling, the archival potential of vesicular microforms has not been established. Library COM applications requiring archival quality duplicates must utilize silver halide print films. However, there are few such applications. Silver halide duplication is otherwise a complicated, expensive, and time-consuming process. Like silver halide camera microfilms, silver halide print films must be exposed and processed in separate operations. They must be handled in darkness and require wet development.

Diazo microfilms feature an emulsion of diazonium salts which are exposed to ultraviolet light transmitted through a master microform, thereby creating a latent image that is subsequently developed with ammonia fumes. The ammonia couples with diazonium salts in areas corresponding to dark areas of the original microform, producing deeply-colored azo dyes. The diazo process thus maintains the polarity of the master microform. In COM applications involving diazo duplication, a special technique called reversal processing is typically used to cause the camera original microform to be of negative polarity, thereby permitting the production of negative diazo duplicates.

As with vesicular microfilms, however, the archival potential of the diazo process has not been established. Although some diazo microforms created twenty years ago remain in good condition, considerable concern has been expressed about the possible fading of diazo images exposed to strong light over time. Broadhurst (1976), in a study completed at the National Reprographic Centre for documentation, reports that diazo microimages fade slowly when exposed to normal levels of actual or simulated ambient light. Fading is accelerated, however, on exposure to the intense light in reader projection systems. Significant information loss may occur in as little as eight hours of constant exposure of a single frame.[2] But, for COM applications that do not require archival quality duplicates -- and most do not -- diazo microfilms offer the advantages of high resolution, resistance to abrasion during heavy use, speed, and convenience.

---

2 It is important to note that diazo microfilms is a generic name that encompasses many brands of film which may vary considerably in their resistance to fading.

Duplicating Equipment

A wide range of equipment is available for the duplication of roll and flat microforms. COM service bureaus generally employ high-speed, high-volume duplicators designed for a production environment. Of greater significance to libraries wishing to make on-demand duplicates of COM masters are the growing number of low-volume, desk-top vesicular and diazo duplicators designed specifically for the production of copies of master microfiche in an office-type environment. Prices for desk-top microfiche duplicators currently range between one thousand and seven thousand dollars. The more expensive models are faster, provide multiple copy capability, and permit semi-automatic operation. Most units will produce developed microfiche copies in less than thirty seconds. Some units will expose and develop two or more fiche simultaneously. All available units are designed for operation by non-technical office personnel. Operator controls and supply replenishment are designed for simplicity. The price per microfiche duplicate is typically in the ten cent range, exclusive of labor and machine amortization or rental.

Low-cost desk-top equipment for roll microforms is not currently available. Roll microform duplication, and high-volume microfiche duplication, is best accomplished on the production-type equipment available at COM service bureaus.

COM Service Bureaus

A COM service bureau is an organization -- usually a private business -- that provides COM recording and duplicating services using a customer's own machine-readable data. Because of the sizeable volume of microform production necessary to justify the high cost of an in-house COM recorder, many COM applications rely on service bureau facilities. For libraries, service bureaus provide an easy way to develop COM applications quickly.

The availability of COM service bureaus, and the range of services they offer, varies with geographical location. Libraries in large metropolitan areas may have a choice of several well-qualified service bureaus. In selecting a COM service bureau, libraries should consider the availability of suitable recording and duplicating equipment, the range of services offered, assurance of quality control over both master and duplicate microforms, reasonable cost, and a record of satisfactory performance, preferably in similar applications. Other factors that are especially meaningful in selecting COM services include turnaround time (the total elapsed time from the delivery of the data to be recorded to the return of required microforms ready for use), the availability of back-up recorders, the level of software support provided to customers during the crucial initial stages of COM production, and staff expertise in both data processing and micrographics. A tour of the service bureau's facilities

prior to conclusion of negotiations is recommended.

COM AS A COMPUTER OUTPUT ALTERNATIVE

COM as Line Printer Replacement

As noted in Section One, the earliest alphanumeric COM recorders were intended to replace line printers in applications requiring the timely production of voluminous printed reports from machine-readable data. Such impact printer replacement applications, remain the largest, and most straight-forward, market for COM. For the production of circulation lists, serials holdings lists, union catalogs, and other batch-processed reports from machine-readable library data bases, COM recorders are invariably faster, generally more versatile, and often more economical than impact printers.

Recording Speed

The most widely-used line printers are impact-type output devices featuring a printing chain consisting of characters represented on embossed metal slugs linked in an endless loop. The chain rotates horizontally at high speed. Paper and an inked ribbon move vertically between the chain and a bank of hammers equal in number to the available print positions. As characters on the chain rotate into their appropriate print positions, individual hammers are activated to impact the paper, thereby driving it against the embossed metal characters.

Since several hammers are activated simultaneously, the device

appears to print entire lines at one time, hence the name.

Other line printers employ drums rather than printing chains.

Basic line printer operation is well-described in a state-of-

the-art review by Wieselman (1977). Despite recent interest

and advances in alternative printing technologies, line

printers remain the most widely-used paper output device.

The rated, or maximum speeds of line printers have

increased over the years to the current high of approximately

2,000 lines per minute. Actual speeds depend on several

factors, including the size of the printable character set,

and may prove significantly lower than rated speeds. The

popular IBM 1403/N3, for example, is rated at 1,500 lines

per minute but actually prints about 1,100 when equipped

with a sixty-four character chain. The effects of larger

character sets are discussed later in this section. Multiple

copies are generally produced on four- or five-ply interleaved

carbon form sets. For copies in excess of form set size,

the print program must be re-executed. Five-ply paper may

reduce the number of re-executions required to produce the

desired number of copies. Four-ply paper, however, is generally

preferred for legibility although the fourth copy itself may

be of questionable quality.

The combination of low actual printing speed and multiple

copy production via carbon paper can result in excessively

long printing times for reports intended for distribution
to many use-points. A two-hundred page, computer-processed
list of items in circulation, to be distributed to twenty
use-points in a multi-branch academic library, will require
five printer runs on four-ply paper. Using the IBM 1403/N3
line printer described above, each run would require twelve
minutes of printing time, plus time for decollating, bursting,
and binding of printed copies. Well over one hour would be
required to complete the entire job.

By way of contrast, COM recorder rated speeds range
between 10,000 and 50,000 lines per minute. Although actual
speeds vary with page lengths and the method of input
preparation, throughput rates of 15,000 to 20,000 lines per
minute are realistic for the faster recorders. A Kodak
KOM-80 or Bell and Howell 3700 COM recorder, for example,
will convert circulation data on an appropriately-formatted
magnetic tape to latent images of two hundred pages of
human-readable information on microfilm or microfiche in
less than two minutes. Allowing time for microfilm processing,
diazo or vesicular duplication, and any additional output
preparation -- such as the insertion of microfilm into
cartridges -- an in-house COM recorder could produce a circulation
list, ready for distribution to twenty use-points, within
half an hour. Even more dramatic throughput improvements
can be achieved with the COM recorder/processors described
in the preceding section.

With its greater speed, a single COM recorder like the
KOM-80 offers output capacity equivalent to about a dozen
line printers -- without a twelve-fold increase in cost.
COM recorder speeds greatly exceed the capabilities of the
Xerox 1200 Computer Printing System, an electrostatic printer
rated at 4,000 lines per minute, and compare favorably with
the IBM 3800 and Honeywell Page Printing System, two non-impact
paper-output devices with printing speeds in excess of 12,000
lines per minute. In replacing line printers with COM
recorders, computing centers and service bureaus translate
increased recording speed into cost savings which can, in
turn, be passed on to libraries and other customers in the
form of lower output charges.

Economy

Several libraries have reported substantial cost reductions
in the conversion of line printer reports to COM. Anderson
(1973) describes such an application at the Los Angeles
Public Library, where a 22,000 page patron directory required
twelve printer runs to produce seventy-one distribution copies.
Conversion to COM saved 82,000 dollars in the first year
with projected subsequent annual savings in the 100,000 dollar
range. While few library applications are so large, proportional
savings have been reported by Simmons (1975), Stecher (1975),
Buckle (1974), Spencer (1973), and Buckle and French (1971).

The several factors that influence the cost-effectiveness of COM applications have, however, seldom been clearly delineated. To set anticipated COM cost savings in perspective, Table 1 compares paper and microfilm output costs for the hypothetical computer-processed circulation list used as an example in the preceding discussion of COM recording speed. The application requires twenty distribution copies of a 200 page report to be produced fifteen times monthly. The cost comparison assumes paper output prepared on four-ply carbon interleaved forms by an IBM 1403/N3 or equivalent line printer equipped with a sixty-four character print chain. The printer is operated by an institutional or commercial computing center or service bureau at a charge of fifty dollars per hour, including decollating and bursting of output. Four-ply paper is priced at thirty dollars per thousand sheets.

Leaving aside discussion of the appropriateness of the microformat and reduction, the analysis of COM costs assumes the use of a service bureau equipped with a minicomputer-controlled COM recorder capable of creating 24:1, sixty-three page microfiche from a library-supplied print-tape. The cost per frame is 2.5 cents. Partial fiche are billed at the rate for sixty-three frames. Duplicate distribution sets, each consisting of four vesicular fiche, are priced at one dollar per set ($.25 per fiche). A modest charge is included for the preparation of a print-tape on the library's host computer.

Table 1

Comparison of Line Printer and 24:1 COM Costs
200 Report Pages, 20 Distribution Points, 15 Updates per Month

---

A. Line Printer Costs

   1. Printing Time: 1 hr @ $50/hr   50.00
   2. 1,000 Sheets of Carbon Forms @ $30/1,000   30.00
                                                               _____
   3. Cost per Line Printer Update   80.00
   4. Monthly Update Frequency   x 15
                                                               _____
       Monthly Line Printer Cost $1200.00

B. COM Microfiche Costs

   1. Preparation of Print Tape   7.50
   2. Production of COM Master Fiche @ .025/frame   6.30
   3. Production of COM Duplicates @ .25/fiche   20.00
                                                               _____
   4. Cost per COM Update   33.80
   5. Monthly Update Frequency   x 15
                                                               _____
   6. Sub-Total: Cost of Monthly Report Production   507.00
   7. Amortization of 20 fiche readers @ $225 each   125.00
   8. Reader Maintenance Allowance   25.00
                                                               _____
       Monthly COM Microfiche Cost $ 657.00

68

While the recording costs given in this example are realistic,
they are subject to considerable local variation and should
not be taken as a measure against which libraries can validly
compare the cost they incur for similar services. Some
libraries may pay a higher per-frame charge for preparation
of an original COM fiche but a lower price for duplicate
fiche.

The itemization of COM costs includes a charge for
microfiche display equipment, lamp replacement, and related
maintenance. The analysis assumes the purchase of twenty
high-quality, desk-top microfiche readers at a price of
225 dollars each. The total purchase price of 4,500 dollars
is conservatively amortized over a three-year useful equipment
life.

In this example, COM's substantial cost advantage is a
factor of report length, frequency of updating, and the number
of required distribution points. As a general rule, COM will
offer a substantial savings over line printer output for long
reports, updated frequently for distribution to many use-points.
To illustrate the interdependence of these three factors,
figure 14 depicts the impact of changes in report update
frequency on the comparison of COM and line printer costs
in the circulation list example. Line printer costs exceed
COM costs beyond three updates per month. The cost differential
widens rapidly with increased update frequency. At five

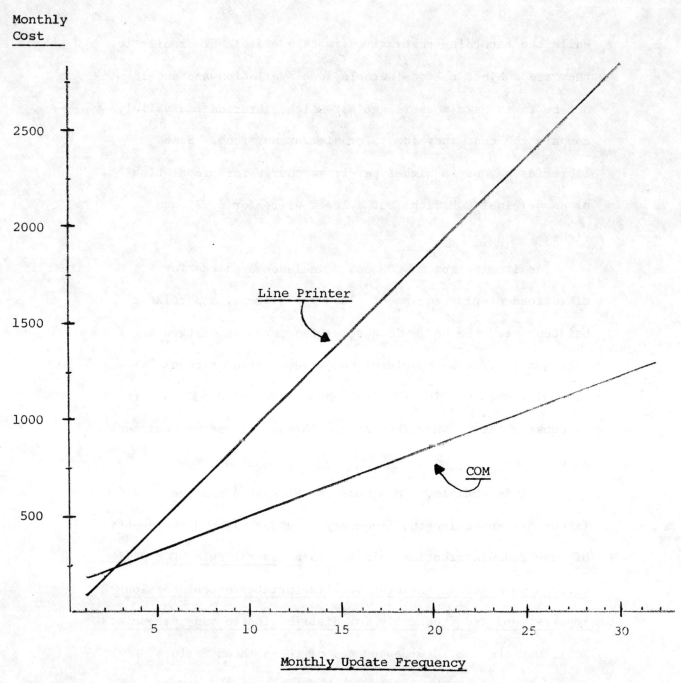

Figure 14
Variations in COM Costs with Monthly Update Frequency

70

updates per month, COM offers a 30% cost reduction. At ten

updates per month, the cost reduction potential increases

to 47.2%. At thirty updates per month, COM reduces output

costs by 58.3%. This example assumes that the two other

determinants of cost-effectiveness -- report length and

number of distribution points -- remain constant at 200

pages and twenty copies respectively.

Figure 15 depicts the impact of changes in the number

of distribution points on the comparison of COM and line

printer costs. Line printer costs exceed COM costs where

the number of distribution points reaches four. As with

update frequency, the cost differential widens rapidly as

the number of distribution points increases. At five

distribution points, COM offers a 33% cost reduction. Cost

reduction potential increases to 45% at ten distribution

points and 59% at thirty distribution points. As indicated

above, it is assumed that report length and update frequency

remain constant at 200 pages and twenty times per month

respectively.

Figure 16 depicts the impact of changes in report length

on the comparison of COM and line printer costs. Assuming

that the number of distribution points and update frequency

remain constant at twenty use points and fifteen times per

month, line printer costs exceed COM costs for reports longer

than about fifty pages. The longer the report, the more the

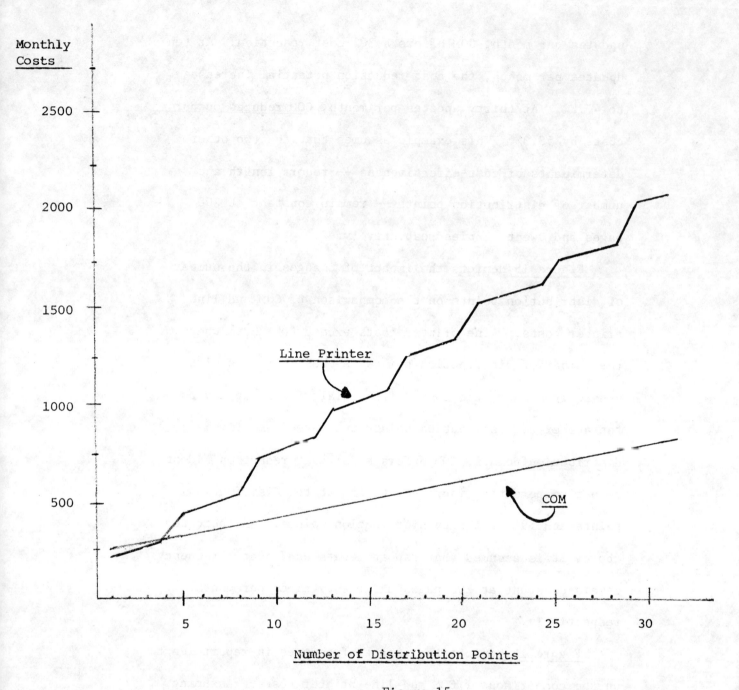

Figure 15

Variations in COM Costs with Number of Distribution Points

72

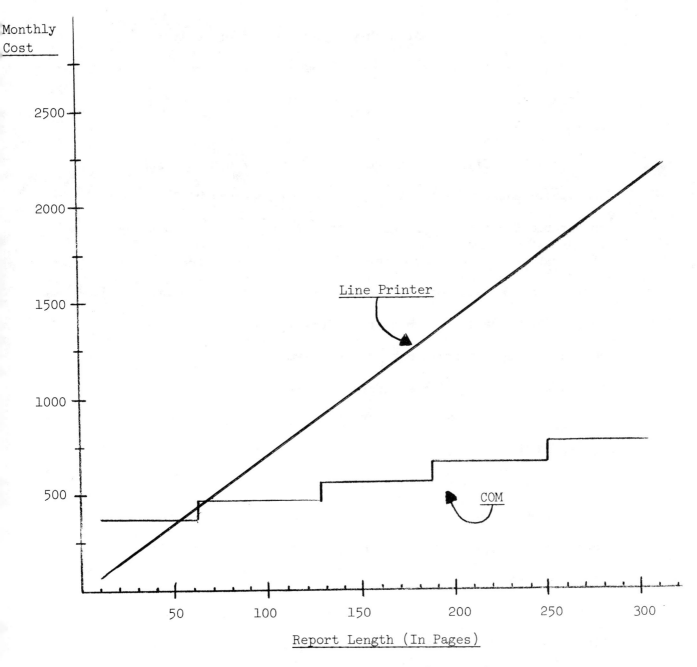

Figure 16
Variations in COM Costs with Report Length

73

comparison favors COM. At eighty pages, COM offers only a 9.5% cost reduction. At 100 pages, the cost reduction potential is 32%. At 300 pages, COM reduces output costs by 60.7%.

All three figures indicate the capacity of COM to respond to significant expansions in reporting requirements without comparable increases in output costs. In figure 14, a doubling of report update frequency from fifteen to thirty times per month offers a 100% improvement in the currency of data with only a 75% increase in COM costs. Line printer costs double with update frequency. In this example, COM offers the advantage of a 25% cost increase avoidance. In figure 15, an increase in the number of distribution points from twenty to thirty provides a 50% increase in the number of places where circulation data can be accessed with only a 35% increase in COM costs. The additional printer time and carbon paper required to produce ten additional line printer report copies would increase output costs by 55.5%. In this instance, COM offers a 20% cost increase avoidance. In figure 16, a 50% increase in report length from 200 to 300 pages is accompanied by only a 21.4% increase in COM costs. Line printer costs would increase 50% with report length. In the case of this expanding report, COM offers a 28.6% cost avoidance advantage.

Output Quality

From the added-value standpoint, COM offers the additional advantage of greatly improved output quality at a significant cost savings. As noted above, the third or fourth copies of a carbon-interleaved form set are typically of fair to marginal quality and utility. All COM duplicates, however, are made directly from the master microform and are of uniform quality.

Printable Character Sets

As noted in the introduction to this section, COM recording offers line printer users the advantage of increased output versatility, especially typographic versatility. Most line printers are equipped with a standard print chain of about sixty-four characters, including the upper-case alphabet, numeric digits, and selected punctuation symbols. This standard printer character set may prove unacceptable for library catalogs and other applications requiring the recording of bibliographic data. Books: A MARC Format (Washington, D.C.: Library of Congress, 1970), defines a printable set of 175 characters. While extended print chains -- the ALA print chain, for example -- have been developed, any expansion of the printable character set necessarily results in a reduction in printing speed. The IBM 1403/N3 line printer, rated at 1,100 lines per minute with a sixty character print chain, will print only about 560 lines per minute with a 120 character chain. The user must weigh the value of enhanced output appearance against this severe reduction in work throughput.

Like line printers, all COM recorders will print the upper-case alphabet, numeric digits, and frequently-used

punctuation symbols. The basic COM character set totals
sixty to seventy characters. Most alphanumeric COM recorders
offer an optional extended set of ninety to 128 characters,
including the lower-case alphabet and additional special
punctuation and mathematical symbols. The 128 character set
is generally considered the minimum required to produce library
catalogs and similar bibliographic products intended for
patron use. Spencer (1973) emphasizes the importance of
upper- and lower-case output in overcoming the reluctance
of COM users in public and academic libraries. The basic
character set furnished with the Cal Comp 2100 Series COM
recorders corresponds to the IBM sixty character PN print
chain, but an optional extended set of 136 characters (fig. 17)
includes the upper and lower case alphabet, six diacritical
marks, twenty-four special characters, and sixteen European
characters. There is a trend toward extended character sets
in newer alphanumeric COM recorders. In some units -- the
3M Beta COM 700H and 700S, for example -- the extended
character set is standard. The DatagraphiX 4550 and 4560
feature a standard set of 128 characters expandable to 160
and 190 characters respectively. By way of contrast, the
older DatagraphiX 4360 could print only sixty-four characters.

Most COM recorder manufacturers will create one or
more special symbols to customer order. Both the Library
of Congress and the New York Public Library have worked with

Standard Set

A-Z	Upper Case Alphabet
0-9	Numeric
	Blank
¢	Cent Sign
.	Period
<	Less Than
(	Left Parenthesis
+	Plus
|	Vertical Stroke
&	Ampersand
■	Erad
!	Exclamation
$	Dollar
*	Asterisk
)	Right Parenthesis
;	Semicolon
¬	Logical NOT
—	Minus
/	Slash
,	Comma
%	Percent
_	Underline
>	Greater Than
?	Question
:	Colon
#	Pound
@	Rate
'	Apostrophe
=	Equal
''	Quote

Total 64 characters

Extended Set

Includes all of the above, plus the following:

Special:

a-z	Lower Case Alphabet
≤	Less Than or Equal
±	Plus or Minus
[	Left Bracket
≥	Greater Than or Equal
]	Right Bracket
≠	Not Equal
∧	Logical AND
∨	Logical OR
↑	Up Arrow
↓	Down Arrow
→	Right Arrow
←	Left Arrow
x	Multiplication
÷	Division
≅	Equivalence
~	Similar
⊂	Subset of
Δ	Delta
¦	Univac
{	Left Brace
}	Right Brace
⌑	Lozonge
\	Reverse Slash

Total 49

Diacritical:

ˇ	Hacek
ˆ	Accent Circumflex
´	Accent acute
¨	Trema (umlaut)
~	Tilde
`	Accent Grave

Total 6

European:

£	English Pound
Ä	Capital A with umlaut
Ü	Capital U with umlaut
Ö	Capital O with umlaut
Ñ	Capital N with tilde
Å	Capital A with circle
Ł	Capital Polish L
Æ	Diagraph AE (upper)
Œ	Diagraph OE (upper)
Ø	Scandinavian O
å	Lower a with circle
ł	Lower polish l
ø	Lower scandinavian o
æ	Diagraph ae (lower)
œ	Diagraph oe (lower)
β	German sz
ç	French c with cedille

Total 17

Figure 17

Extended COM Character Set
(Courtesy: California Computer Products, Inc.)

COM service bureaus to develop extended character sets

containing special diacritical marks and other symbols essential

to the recording of bibliographic data in a large research

library. Malinconico (1976, 1977) provides an excellent

disucssion of the nature of these extended character sets.

The ease with which special symbols can be created, as noted

in Section Two, depends on the method of character generation

employed in the recording process. Character set changes

or additions in DatagraphiX alphanumeric COM recorders require

modification or replacement of the character-forming matrix

located in the neck of the Charactron[TM] CRT. Character set

expansion in dot matrix recorders is necessarily limited

by matrix size -- the greater the number of available light

points, the greater the character-forming capability. The

Memorex 1603, with its five by seven dot matrix, will print

only sixty-four characters. The Quantor 105, 3M Beta COM

700S, and Bell and Howell 3700 employ a larger six by

nine or seven by ten matrix to produce extended character

sets. Character set expansion in stroke-generation alphanumeric

COM recorders, such as the Kodak KOM-80 or 3M EBR, is

technically simple, requiring a hardware change consisting

of a minor modification of character-generating circuitry.

Graphic COM recorders, like the Information International

FR-80 or Cal Comp 1675, also create individual characters

by stroke-generation from pre-stored definitions. The FR-80,

for example, stores from 128 to 242 character definitions.
As in stroke-generation alphanumeric COM recorders, these
character definitions are represented in hardware, but, in
graphic COM recorders, an essentially unlimited character
set can be generated through software modification. The
generation of characters through software is, however, much
slower than hardware generation.

The 3M EBR will print fifteen Greek symbols useful in
mathematical applications, but large research libraries and
smaller specialized collections may require entire non-Roman
alphabets. The Cal Comp 2100 and DatagraphiX 4500 Series
COM recorders offer optional Japanese Katakana character
sets (fig. 18). DatagraphiX also offers a Cyrillic character
set and will create Charactron^{TM} matrices, to customer order,
for virtually any language. COM manufacturers doing business
in Eastern Europe and the Middle East have produced recorders
with Arabic and Farsi character sets.

As might be expected, the increased cost of the hardware
and software required to develop the extended character sets
essential to the printing of bibliographic data necessitates
higher prices on the part of service bureaus equipped with
such special COM recorders. Malinconico (1977) cites frame
prices in the range 4.5 to 9.3 cents for extended character
set work. Table 2 considers the impact of a 9.3 cent per
frame recording charge on the hypothetical library circulation

Figure 18
Japanese Katakana Matrix
(Courtesy: DatagraphiX, Inc.)

Table 2

Comparison of Line Printer and COM Costs
for Extended Character Set Work
200 Report Pages, 20 Distribution Points, 15 Updates per Month

A. **Line Printer Costs**

1.	Printing Time: 2 hrs @ $50/hr	100.00
2.	1,000 Sheets of Carbon Forms @ $30/1,000	30.00
3.	Cost per Line Printer Update	130.00
4.	Monthly Update Frequency	x 15
	Monthly Line Printer Costs	$1850.00

B. **COM Microfiche Costs**

1.	Preparation of Print Tape	7.50
2.	Production of COM Master Fiche @ .093/frame	23.40
3.	Production of COM Duplicates @ .25/fiche	20.00
4.	Cost per COM Update	50.90
5.	Monthly Update Frequency	x 15
6.	Sub-Total: Cost of Monthly Report Production	763.50
7.	Amortization of 20 fiche readers @ $225 each	125.00
8.	Reader Maintenance Allowance	25.00
	Monthly COM Microfiche Costs	$ 913.50

list application presented earlier in this section. The cost
comparison assumes that the application requires printing
of the upper- and lower-case Roman alphabet plus selected
special symbols similar to those depicted in figure 17.
Other application parameters remain as previously presented.
The report length is 200 pages. Twenty distribution points
are required. Update frequency is fifteen times per month.

Note that, as described above, the extended print chain
decreases line printer speed by a half and doubles printing
cost. COM costs, however, increase in only a relatively
minor area -- the production of COM master fiche. The cost
of print-tape preparation, fiche duplication, and display
equipment remain unchanged. While, in Table 1, COM reduced
output costs by 51.3% in an application requiring upper-case
printing only, Table 2 demonstrates a potential 54.9% savings
over extended character set output produced by a line printer.
Greater savings would be realized with increases in report
length, update frequency, the number of distribution points,
or the size of the character set to be printed.

Type Face, Size, and Intensity

A primary goal in COM type face design is to preserve
legibility, often through several generations of duplicates, while
striving for compatibility with optical character recognition
(OCR) equipment. While there is no standard COM type face,

the National Micrographics Association (1976) recommends,

and many COM manufacturers employ, the European Computer

Manufacturers' Association's OCR-B Alphanumeric Character

Set, which is also available in an IBM Selectric element for

typing source documents. Other popular sans serif type faces

include Gothic, used in the Bell and Howell 3700 and 3800

COM recorders, and the NMA Microfont, one of three type

faces that are standard and interchangeable with the Information

International FR-80 recorder. Where typographic quality is

essential, the Information International COMp80, an enhanced

version of the powerful FR-80 designed for rapid and economical

photocomposition of lists subject to frequent change, will

print the three COM type faces offered with the FR-80;

additional Roman, Gothic, italic, and utility type faces

commonly used in technical publications; and over three

hundred graphic arts type faces. COM and utility type faces

are created by the minimum number of strokes necessary to

shape individual characters. Graphic arts type faces are

painted as a series of vertical strokes. Recorder software

permits the interchange of type faces within a single microimage.

The use of graphic arts type faces, however, greatly reduces

recording speed.

While the simplest alphanumeric COM recorders, like their

line printer counterparts, can print characters in only one

size and intensity, the 3M Beta COM 700H will print the Times

Roman type face in four intensities. The Bell and Howell 3700
and 3800 will record characters at fifteen percent larger than
regular size. Users of the Kodak KOM-80 can select regular,
bold, italic, or italic bold characters. Graphic recorders
again offer the greatest type size versatility. The Applicon
AP75 Micrographic Plotter, for example, offers an optional
hardware character generator that will print eight character
sizes, from six to thirty-two points. The Information
International COMp80 will print graphic arts characters in
sixty-four sizes from four to thirty-two points. Through
software, sizes can be varied within a microimage -- an
important feature that permits, for example, the printing
of the main entry portion of catalog data in one size and
the collation and tracings portion in a smaller size.

Page Formatting

As noted earlier, the most prevalent COM page format
emulates an eleven by fourteen inch computer printout page
consisting of sixty-four lines of up to 132 characters each.
Certain COM recorders, however, permit modifications in this
basic format. For greater information compaction, the number
of lines per page can be increased to seventy-two by the
Cal Comp 2100 Series COM recorders; to eighty-six by the
Bell and Howell 3700; to eighty-eight by the Kodak KOM-85
and DatagraphiX 4500 Series recorders; or to 102 by the Kodak
Komstar recorders. The number of characters per line can
be increased to 160 by the Bell and Howell 3700 and DatagraphiX
4500 Series COM recorders. The Kodak KOM-85 will record 172

characters per line. When equipped with an optional five by seven matrix, the Kodak Komstar is capable of recording 207 characters per line.

Alternatively, line lengths can be reduced to eighty characters, producing the equivalent of an 8.5 by 11 inch document image and increasing the number of images on a standard microfiche to ninety-eight (in seven rows and fourteen columns) at 24:1 effective reduction; 325 (in thirteen rows and twenty-five columns) at 42:1; and 420 (in fifteen rows and twenty-eight columns) at 48:1. At 24:1, the 8.5 by 11 inch imaginary document results in a COM microfiche format that is compatible with the NMA standard for source documents.

For 16mm roll microfilm applications, the 3M EBR has a variable frame advance that allows users to significantly increase information compaction by reducing the gap between frames. When imaginary eleven by fourteen inch documents are recorded at 24:1 effective reduction, the normal advance leaves a gap of 5.4mm between cine-mode frames and permits slightly less than two thousand microimages per one hundred foot roll. By reducing the gap to .6mm, for example, an additional eight hundred frames can be recorded. In the comic-mode, the width of frames can be reduced to accommodate catalog card images and other bibliographic data formatted in lines of less than 132 characters. This flexibility permits the expansion of library catalogs and other dynamic data bases without unduly increasing the number of rolls, cartridges, or cassettes the user must handle.

On both roll microfilm or microfiche, several COM recorders

have the ability to enhance information compaction

by eliminating space between frames altogether. This technique,

called scrolling, presents information on cine-mode 16mm

microfilm or in microfiche columns as a continuous series of

lines. Scrolling is used effectively in several COM-generated

bibliographic products including the Georgia Tech Library's

LENDS microfiche catalog, described by Greene (1975a), and

MARCFICHE, a MARC-derivative bibliographic service produced

by MARC Applied Research, Incorporated (fig. 19).

Within frames on roll microfilm or microfiche, the 3M

Beta COM recorders provide a number of special page-formatting

facilities including proportional spacing, underlining,

overlining, subscripting, and superscripting. The extensive

formatting software of the Information International COMp80

permits both fixed and proportional spacing, ragged or justified

right margins, automatic centering, and columnar printing.

COM vs. On-Line Systems

In addition to functioning as a line printer replacement

for the production of batch-processed, computer-generated

reports, COM represents a viable, economical alternative

to on-line systems in library applications without real-time

information requirements. Where the real-time requirement

is modest, COM can be utilized as one information storage

```
---------------------------- 527101 -----------
International Abolitionist Federation.
  Compte-rendu du congres; [annuel] [v.p.]
  illus. 23 cm.
  Vols. for <1899, 1927> issued under its French
name: Federation abolitionniste internationale.
  1.Prostitution--Societies, etc.
HQ106.I33                                11-33782
---------------------------- 527102 -----------
California. Division of Bay Toll Crossings.
Richmond-San Rafael Bridge.
  Annual report.  [Sacramento]
  illus. 28 cm.  1st-  1953-
  First report covers the period Feb. 26 to
Sept. 1, 1953.
  Reports for 1953-   issued by the Division
under its earlier name: Division of San
Francisco Bay Toll Crossings.
  1.Richmond-San Rafael Bridge.
HE376.R55C26a    624.7                   55-31251
---------------------------- 527103 -----------
Agrartudomanyi Egyetem. Erdomernoki Kar, Sopron.
  Agrartudomanyi Egyetem Erdomernoki Karanak
evkonyve.  Sopron.
  illus. 25 cm.  t. 1, fasc. 1. 1950.
  Title also in Latin.
  Articles summarized in Russian and usually in
German.
  1.Forests and forestry--Collected works.
2.Forest ecology--Collected works.
3.Forests and forestry--Hungary--Collected
works.  I.Erdeszettudomanyi kozlemenyek
SD1.A33a                                 56-33938
---------------------------- 527104 -----------
You--and the world of work. [Filmstrip]  Audio
Visual Narrative Arts, 1975.  4 filmstrips.
color. 35 mm. and 4 phonodiscs (2 s. each; for
manual or automatic projectors), 12 in., 33 1/3
rpm.
  Also issued with phonotape in cassette.
  With teacher's guide.
  Script, Wendy Rydell; narration, Jack Dahlby,
Doug Weathers, Linda Fields; consultant,
Rochelle P. Herlich; photography, William T.
Martin.
  Provides information on various occupations,
aids in selecting a career, and explains how to
obtain and hold a job.
  CONTENTS: 1. Getting to know you. 54 fr., 6
min.-- 2. Choosing your career. 59 fr., 10 min.-
- 3. Getting a job. 59 fr., 9 min.-- 4. Keeping
the job. 61 fr., 9 min.
  1.Vocational guidance.  2.Job vacancies.
I.Audio Visual Narrative Arts (Firm)
HF5381           371.4                   75-735829
---------------------------- 527105 -----------
Marijuana update: its use and abuse. [Filmstrip]
  Audio Visual Narrative Arts, 1975.  4
filmstrips. color. 35 mm. and 4 phonodiscs (2 s.
each; for manual or automatic projectors), 12
in., 33 1/3 rpm.
  Also issued with phonotape in cassette.
  With teacher's guide.
  Script, Wendy Rydell; photography, Brian
McDermott.
  Investigates the history of the use of
marihuana, the physical and psychological
effects on the user, and medical uses of the
drug and suggests the need for a reappraisal of
laws pertaining to the control of marihuana use.
  CONTENTS: 1. Marihuana and man. 77 fr., 13
min.-- 2. Marihuana and the user. 75 fr., 13
min.-- 3. Marihuana and the drug culture. 82
fr., 13 min.-- 4. Marihuana and the law. 75 fr.,
16 min.
  1.Marihuana.  2.Drugs--Physiological effect.
3.Drugs--Psychological aspects.  4.Drugs--Laws
and legislation.  I.Audio Visual Narrative Arts
(Firm)
HV5822.M3        362.2                    75-735830
```

Figure 19
Scrolled Page Format
(Courtesy: MARC Applied Research, Inc.)

medium in an economical hybrid system that combines microform

displays with CRT or printing terminals. Where real-time

information is essential, COM can provide continued access

to important data in the event of on-line system failure.

COM as an On-Line System Alternative

There is an obvious and direct relationship between the

accuracy of information and its value. In transaction-oriented

applications -- such as library circulation control, acquisitions,

and cataloging -- the accuracy of information depends on its

currency. In batch-oriented computer systems, data reflecting

the occurrence of a given transaction is processed and reported

some time after the transaction itself. In a batch-oriented

computerized circulation system, for example, the machine-readable

master circulation file is updated, and circulation lists

printed, on a pre-determined schedule. In such systems, the

currency of reported information depends on the frequency

of file updates and report production. Because batch-processed

reports cannot reflect transactions occurring in the intervals

between file updates, a circulation list produced fifteen

times per month can be used with greater confidence than one

produced five times.

Because of the relative slowness of line printers, computer

centers and service bureaus may not be able to schedule and

guarantee the frequent and timely production of the very long

reports characteristic of many library applications. In some cases, sufficient printer time may not be available. Veaner

(1974) has further noted that libraries have rarely been

accorded priority status by the computer centers that serve

them. Academic computer centers in particular may be

uninterested in the relatively straightforward, output-oriented

applications characteristic of library automation. Faced with

the inability to obtain printer output on an acceptable schedule,

libraries requiring access to computer-processed data that is

no more than a specified number of hours old may turn to an

on-line, real-time information system. In such a system, a

machine-readable circulation or other data file is maintained

on magnetic disk, drum, or other direct access storage device.

Unlike off-line systems which batch transaction data for

processing against a master file at pre-scheduled intervals,

real-time systems post transactions to the master file as

they occur. File updating is simultaneous with the event

rather than occurring at some time later than the transactions

it records. Using a remote display or printing terminal,

the master file can be examined on demand with assurance

that the information it contains reflects the most recent

transactions.

While on-line, real-time systems offer the advantage of currency, with its implied accuracy, they can be very expensive. Although prices are dropping steadily, disk and drum storage still cost more than the magnetic tape used for master files in batch-oriented systems. Actual storage costs will vary from one computer installation to another and depend heavily on local accounting practices. Malinconico (1977) suggests a charge of $10,000 per month for a file of two million bibliographic records maintained in direct-access storage. On-line access requires a terminal at every use point. Programming requirements for on-line, real-time systems are complex, with long development times. In many applications, printed reports are still required to provide information during times when the computer is down or otherwise unavailable.

To minimize costs in applications where currency of information is important but access to up-to-the-minute information is not essential, COM can be used to produce batch-processed reports at more frequent intervals than would be possible with slower line printing equipment or other paper output devices. With their greater output speed, COM recorders can produce long reports several times daily, providing the user with information that is no more than a few hours old in the worst case. COM's demonstrable cost advantages, detailed above, permit significant increases in report production frequency without comparable increases in cost. Figure 11, above, indicates that, for approximately the same expenditure, the hypothetical 200-page circulation report could be distributed to twenty use-points thirty times per month on microfiche or twelve times per month in paper form. COM report production at half-day, or possibly more frequent intervals, would not approach the costs of an on-line, real-time system for an application of this size.

COM in a Hybrid System

While many applications can be satisfied with information that is no more than one-half day old, on-line real-time systems may offer superior performance in fulfilling certain information management requirements. On-line, real-time access to a machine-readable library catalog, for example, provides the user with information about the most recently acquired and cataloged items. Batch-processed holdings lists, as noted above, cannot reflect items acquired and cataloged in the interval between report printings. Some libraries consider access to the most recent machine-readable records an essential feature of a computer-based catalog. In such cases, COM can interface with on-line, real-time access in an economical hybrid system.

As an example, the heart of such a hybrid system would consist of a COM-generated catalog reflecting the library's holdings at the time the catalog was printed. New items are added to a machine-readable disk or drum file as they are cataloged. At pre-determined intervals, these new items are batch-processed against a master catalog file on magnetic tape and an updated COM catalog produced, duplicated, and distributed. Cataloging information prepared in the interval between catalog updates is fully accessible on disk or drum via remote terminal. The user seeking information about a particular item would first consult the COM catalog. Failing to find it there, the disk or drum file would be consulted to determine whether the desired item had been acquired since the catalog was printed. Users seeking information about very recent imprints would circumvent the COM catalog and consult the new item file first. The system is more economical than a completely on-line system in two ways:

1. The required amount of expensive disk or
    drum storage is reduced. A minicomputer
    located in the library might be used for
    the on-line file of newly cataloged items,
    with batch-processing and COM catalog
    production occurring at a remote computer
    center or service bureau.

2. Because most information needs will be
    satisfied by consulting the COM catalog,

fewer printing or display terminals will
be required. Although prices have come
down, terminals remain from five to upwards
of twenty times more expensive than
microfiche readers.

Such hybrid systems permit many variations. An entire
brief entry catalog might be maintained on-line with full
bibliographic information available on COM-generated microfilm
or microfiche. The brief entry catalog would require less
disk or drum storage. Alternatively, an author/title catalog
might be accessible on-line in its entirety with subject and
classified catalogs printed via COM. Such an approach both
reduces direct access storage requirements and eliminates
the complex task of programming an on-line subject-access
application.

COM as On-Line System Back-Up

On-line information systems are vulnerable to hardware
malfunction. Such malfunction may occur at either the central
processing facility or at the remote terminal site. Hardware
malfunction typically results in the partial or complete
unavailability of machine-readable files. In the case of
library catalogs and other applications where the continued
availability of information is essential to daily operation,
COM can serve as a relatively inexpensive back-up information

storage medium. COM can also serve a useful back-up function in applications where limitations on available disk or drum storage do not permit the continuous maintenance of large data bases on-line.

Because silver halide microforms, when properly processed and stored, have archival potential, COM is an appropriate medium for the long-term preservation of information. Periodic recording of library data bases on microfilm, combined with off-site storage of COM masters, can form the basis of an effective, but inexpensive, protection program for library catalogs and other vital operating records.

Limitations of COM

COM shares some of the limitations of microforms produced from source documents. A reader is required. Microimages cannot be annotated. User resistance may accompany the elimination of paper reports. As already indicated, COM is generally not cost-effective for short or infrequently updated reports with few distribution points. Likewise, reports that are divided into separate parts for the use of various individuals may be best retained in paper. Paper output is generally preferred in applications requiring frequent reference between two pages or the comparison of pages from two or more reports.

The extent to which any or all of these factors will limit systems design is situational-dependent and must be

carefully analyzed. Where the ability to write on report
pages is essential, for example, COM should be avoided.
Where the potential for significant cost reduction exists,
however, the librarian should closely examine the necessity
of stated requirements that constrain systems change.

SECTION FOUR

COM SYSTEMS DESIGN

Output Selection

As described in Section Two, most available COM recorders
now will produce either 16mm roll microfilm or 105mm microfiche
at several effective reductions. The choice of microform and
effective reduction can favorably or adversely affect the
utility of a COM system and requires careful consideration.

Roll Microforms vs. Microfiche

Roll microform is a generic term for reel microfilm,
microfilm cartridges, and microfilm cassettes. Reel microfilm --
the simplest and least expensive microform to create -- consists
of processed 16mm or 35mm microfilm wound onto a flanged
plastic holder. Film lengths vary, 100 and 215 feet being
the most common.

Reel microfilm offers two broad advantages: 1) unitization
and 2) file sequence integrity. With its high image capacity
per unit, reel microfilm is well-suited to the unitization
of library catalogs and other very long reports. The capacity
of a 100 foot reel of 16mm- COM-generated microfilm depends
on image orientation and filming format but generally exceeds
2,000 computer printout page-images reduced 24:1. Longer film
and/or higher effective reductions will significantly increase

reel capacity. Long reports will often fit on a single reel.
In addition, the sequence of microimages and report units on
film is fixed and cannot be inadvertently altered by the user.

Despite these strengths, reel microfilm suffers several
serious disadvantages that limit its utility in many COM
applications. Most significantly, it can prove difficult to
use in applications requiring rapid reference to microimages
on several reels. The necessity of removing a reel of microfilm
from its container, mounting it with more or less difficulty
on a reader, threading the proper amount of leader through
the film gate, rewinding the film, and returning the reel to
its proper container when finished constitute both a genuine
inconvenience and a potentially insurmountable psychological
obstacle to many users. Difficulties in film handling can,
however, be minimized in several ways. Multiple readers can
be employed at each location, for example. Alternatively,
the Information Design ROM-3 COM Terminal and LCR 1100, marketed
by Autographics, can eliminate multiple reels and consequent
film handling by displaying microimages from a captive 16mm
reel containing up to 1,200 feet of vesicular film. The
special reel remains inside the reader and is not touched by
the user (fig. 20). The greater film length capacity increases
the likelihood that a library catalog or other long report
will fit on a single reel.

Figure 20
Autographics Reader showing Large 16mm Reel
(Courtesy: Micrographics Equipment Review)

Cartridges and cassettes represent a more conventional

solution for users who want the high image capacity of reel

microfilm without the inconvenience of manual film handling.

While they share a common purpose, cartridges and cassettes

differ in design and function. A cartridge (fig. 21) is a

plastic, single-core microfilm container. When mounted on an

appropriate reader, microfilm from the cartridge is automatically

threaded onto a take-up spool built into the reader itself.

The microfilm passes out of the cartridge during use and must

be rewound into the cartridge prior to removal from the reader.

A cassette (fig. 22) is a plastic, double-core microfilm

container that encloses both a supply spool and a take-up

spool in a single housing. Cassettes require no film threading

and can be removed from the reader at any time without rewinding.

As with cartridges, a special reader is required.

Spreitzer (1972) provides a detailed discussion of the

various cartridges and cassettes available to libraries.

Librarians responsible for COM systems design should be aware

that most available cartridges are incompatible and cannot be

used with readers manufactured by competitors. The choice of

the cartridges of one supplier necessarily limits future systems

change and equipment selection. The same incompatibility

prevails among cassette manufacturers. Cartridges and cassettes

are themselves incompatible.

Figure 21
A 16mm Microfilm Cartridge
(Courtesy: 3M Company)

Figure 22
A 16mm Microfilm Cassette
(Courtesy: Memorex Corporation)

While the lack of standardization undoubtedly deters
the development of cartridge and cassette applications, the
relatively high cost of roll microform readers may have an
even greater impact on the selection of an appropriate
COM-generated microform. Table 3 recosts the hypothetical
circulation list application presented in Section Three,
Table 1, utilizing microfilm cartridges rather than microfiche
as the output medium. While some savings are realized
through the lower cost of producing roll microforms, the
apparently modest loading charge of two dollars per cartridge,
when incurred fifteen times monthly for a set of twenty
cartridges, results in a substantial increase in the cost of
producing the COM update. The most substantial increase in
total system costs, however, is derived from the high cost of
cartridge readers. Roll microform readers are invariably
more expensive than microfiche readers. In this hypothetical
application, projected cartridge system costs exceed line
printer costs by about 200 dollars per month. An increase in
report length, update frequency, or the number of distribution
points would be necessary to justify the conversion of paper
output to microfilm in cartridges on the basis of cost alone.
Use of a less expensive cartridge or cassette reader would
favorably affect COM costs, but such readers are few in number
and may lack the quality required in public-use applications.
Library applications employing roll microforms as an economical

Table 3

Comparison of Cartridge and Microfiche Costs
200 Report Pages, 20 Distribution Points, 15 Updates per Month

A. Microfiche Costs

1.	Preparation of Print Tape	7.50
2.	Production of COM Master Fiche @ .025/frame	6.30
3.	Production of COM Duplicates @ .25/fiche	20.00
4.	Cost per COM Update	33.80
5.	Monthly Update Frequency	x 15
6.	Sub-Total: Cost of Monthly Report Production	507.00
7.	Amortization of 20 fiche readers @ $225 each	125.00
8.	Reader Maintenance Allowance	25.00
	Monthly Microfiche Total	$ 657.00

B. Cartridge Costs

1.	Preparation of Print Tape	7.50
2.	Production of COM Master Film @ .02/frame	4.00
3.	Production of COM Duplicates @ .0035/frame	14.00
4.	Cartridge Loading @ $2.00/cartridge	40.00
5.	Cost per COM Update	65.50
6.	Monthly Update Frequency	x 15
7.	Sub-Total: Cost of Monthly Report Production	982.50
8.	Amortization of 20 Cartridge Readers @ $1000 each	555.00
9.	Reader Maintenance Allowance	25.00
10.	Amortization of 1 yr supply of cartridges @ $2.00 each	3.30
	Monthly Cartridge Total	$1565.80

alternative to line printer output are generally characterized by a very large number of distribution points. The obvious example is a library system's union catalog, several copies of which may be distributed to each participating library.

The availability of a wide selection of high-quality microfiche readers in the 200 to 300 dollar price range argues persuasively for microfiche as the microform of choice in the hypothetical circulation list application and others like it. Most librarians are familiar with microfiche as a rectangular sheet of film containing multiple microimages in a two-dimensional grid pattern of rows and columns. Although microfiche are available in several sizes, the 105mm and 148mm (approximately four by six inch) fiche is the American and international standard for COM as for source documents. As noted in Section Two, the several standard image capacities depend on three commonly-used effective reductions: 24:1, 42:1, and 48:1. The rapid development of American and international microfiche standards has helped to encourage equipment manufacturers to build relatively inexpensive readers. Even the lowest priced models have features previously offered only on very expensive roll microform equipment.

From the systems design standpoint, microfiche offers the additional advantage of semi-random retrieval. Roll microforms limit the user to serial access to desired information. Once the appropriate reel or cartridge is correctly mounted on

a reader, the user seeking a particular microimage must pass
through all preceding microimages. Access time depends on
the location of the desired microimage relative to the start
of the film. In reel and cartridge systems, the average access
time equals the time required to traverse one-half the film-
length plus the time required to rewind one-half the film-length.[3]
Readers with motorized film advances can reduce the traverse
time to desired microimages but, as will be discussed later
in this section, such readers are more complex and expensive
than their manual counterparts. By way of contrast, microfiche
users can access a given fiche in a manual or automated file
directly, without examining preceding fiche. Access to a specific
item of information within a fiche may still, to a degree, require
serial examination of microimages. Fiche indexing, described
later in this section, can minimize such serial examination.

Because most prevailing COM microfiche formats do not
accommodate more than 270 computer printout page-images, a
library catalog or long report will occupy several or many
fiche. Some COM systems designers have expressed concern that
fiche location and refiling problems may be a concommitant
of such applications, especially where the fiche are intended
for use by a public who have had minimal instruction. Several
suppliers offer tray-type files for the desk-top organization
and storage of COM fiche. Such trays typically hold several

---

[3] This formula does not apply to readers that eliminate
rewinding through the use of cassettes or captive reels.

hundred fiche, possibly separated by tabbed dividers. The user,

however, must flip through individual fiche until the desired

microform is located. For very active COM applications, panel-type

storage units can eliminate much time-consuming fiche handling.

Panel-type files (fig. 23) consist of a paper or plastic housing

with pockets into which individual fiche or jackets are inserted

upright, titles visible. The inclusive contents of particular

fiche are immediately apparent as are fiche sequence numbers

used in refiling. Empty panel pockets indicate refiling locations.

Individual file sections can be further highlighted through the

use of colored panels and side tabs. The capacity of individual

double-sided panels ranges from twenty to eighty fiche, depending

on panel size and pocket spacing. The panels themselves can be

stored in binders or mounted on desk-stands, rotary carousels,

or wall racks. The largest available configurations will hold

more than 7,000 fiche. The panels also protect fiche from dust

and warping. The fiche themselves can be color-striped for

identification and misfile protection.

Low vs. High Reduction

As already noted, the most widely used COM reductions are

24:1, 42:1, and 48:1. As the standard source document microfiche

reduction, 24:1 was selected for the COM edition of Library of

Congress Subject Headings, Eighth Edition to facilitate use

with existing library display equipment. From the systems

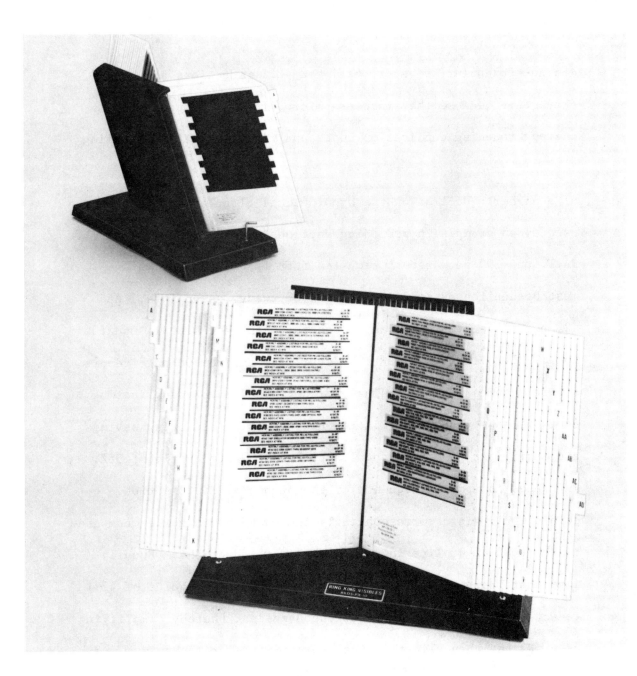

Figure 23
Panel-Type Filing for Microfiche
(Courtesy: Ring King Visibles)

107

design standpoint, however, 42:1 and 48:1 reductions are more

attractive because they increase microform image capacity,

thereby reducing duplication costs and minimizing fiche handling

for data bases of a given size. Table 4 indicates the impact

of a higher reduction on the hypothetical circulation list

used as an example in preceding sections of this report. At

24:1, the 200 page report requires four fiche, each of which

must be duplicated for distribution to twenty use-points. At

.25 per fiche, the duplicating costs for fifteen monthly updates

total 300 dollars. At 42:1, however, the entire 200 page report

can be accommodated on a single fiche. The monthly duplicating

costs will be reduced by 75% to just $75. The resulting savings

are sufficient to reduce total application costs by almost 35%.

Increases in update frequency or the number of distribution

points would yield correspondingly increased savings when compared

to the cost of duplicating fiche at lower reductions. Equally

important from the systems design standpoint, the choice of 42:1

reduction will eliminate microfiche handling, thereby simplifying

use. Rather than selecting the appropriate microfiche from

among four, the user need only consult a reader with a single

fiche pre-mounted and ready for viewing. It should be noted,

however, that dust and scratches are more likely to obscure

data on higher reduction microforms.

Table 4

Comparison of COM Fiche Costs at 24:1 and 42:1 Reductions
200 Report Pages, 20 Distribution Points, 15 Updates per Month

A. 24:1 Costs

1.	Preparation of Print Tape	7.50
2.	Preparation of COM Master Fiche @ .025/frame	6.30
3.	Production of COM Duplicates @ .25/fiche	20.00
4.	Cost per COM Update	33.80
5.	Monthly Update Frequency	x 15
6.	Sub-Total: Cost of Monthly Report Production	507.00
7.	Amortization of 20 Fiche Readers @ $225 each	125.00
8.	Reader Maintenance Allowance	25.00
	Monthly 24:1 Costs	$ 657.00

B. 42:1 Costs

1.	Preparation of Print Tape	7.50
2.	Preparation of COM Master Fiche @ .025/frame	6.30
3.	Production of COM Duplicates @ .25/fiche	5.00
4.	Cost per COM Update	18.80
5.	Monthly Update Frequency	x 15
6.	Sub-Total: Cost of Monthly Report Production	282.00
7.	Amortization of 20 Fiche Readers @ $225 each	125.00
8.	Reader Maintenance Allowance	25.00
	Monthly 42:1 Costs	$ 432.00

COM Display Equipment

The use of COM-generated roll microfilm or microfiche requires a reader or other display device. Well-selected display equipment is crucial to the success of library COM applications and constitutes the single most important factor in overcoming user resistance. Guidelines for the selection of microform readers for libraries have been developed and presented by a number of organizations and individuals, including LaHood (1977); Hawken (1975); the National Microfilm Association (1974); the Library Technology Program (1973); Barrett (1972); Sherman (1972); and Wright (1970). These guidelines, developed mainly for source document microforms, merely establish minimum expectations and are reviewed here only as they apply to the evaluation of COM readers for library applications. Such evaluation must deal with technical and human factors considerations as well as application requirements.

Display Methods

A microform reader is a projection device that magnifies microimages so they can be read with the unaided eye. Micrographics terminology distinguishes readers from viewers, which are hand-held magnifiers that operate with ambient light or a battery-powered light source. While viewers permit convenient reference to microforms by field engineers and technical personnel in locations where power required for other display systems is unavailable, they are of little utility in library COM applications.

All available COM readers employ one of two display methods. Front projection readers (figs. 24, 25) display magnified microimages onto an opaque surface. While a few portable front-projection readers display microimages on a table-top, the viewing surface in most of the COM readers offered to libraries is built into the reader itself. Rear projection readers (figs. 26, 27) direct magnified microimages onto the back of a translucent screen which the user views from the front. A comparative performance analysis by Judisch (1968) failed to demonstrate the superiority of either display method. Rear projection readers, however, are typically preferred in applications where room light cannot be optimized for microform display. This is often the case with library COM applications -- a COM-generated circulation list located at a library information desk is one example. A COM catalog located in a brightly lit area formerly devoted to a card catalog is another. While the ambient light falling on a front projection screen may be reflected back at the user, thereby interfering with the displayed microimage, much of the ambient light falling on a rear projection screen is absorbed inside the reader itself. Several newer front projection readers, however, employ clear plastic filters to shield the screen. In both front and rear projection COM readers, much of the adverse effect of ambient light can be minimized with a hood.

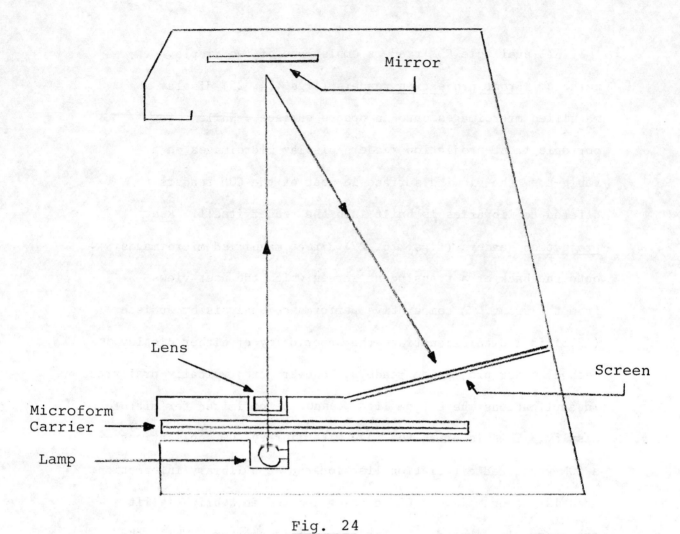

Fig. 24

Schematic Drawing of Front Projection Optical Path

Figure 25
Front-Projection COM Reader
(Courtesy: Realist, Inc.)

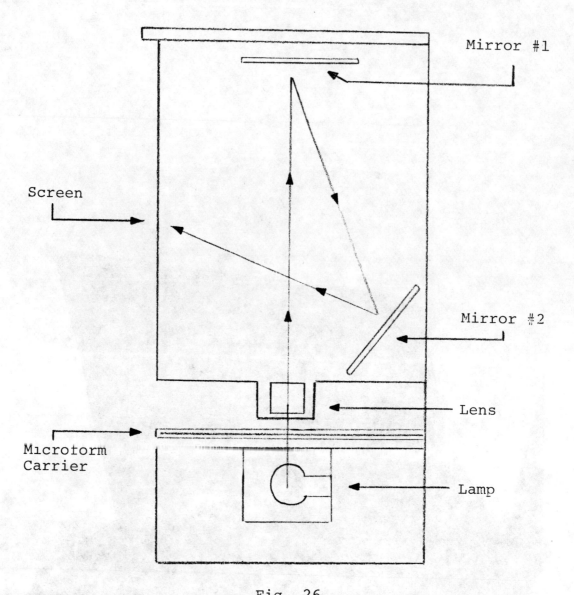

Fig. 26

Schematic Drawing of Rear Projection Optical Path

Figure 27
Rear-Projection COM Reader
(Courtesy: Realist, Inc.)

115

Image Quality

Regardless of display method, reader image quality is
evaluated in terms of resolution, contrast, and freedom from
distortion. Resolution refers to the ability of a reader's
optical system and screen to render fine details visible.
Reader resolution can be determined subjectively by examining
the displayed microimage of a filmed test target consisting
of closely spaced numbered lines of decreasing size. The
National Bureau of Standards Microcopy 101A Resolution Test
Target is the most widely used in the United States for this
purpose. Many librarians, however, will find that the resulting
numerical expression of resolution is not very helpful in
assessing the legibility of a displayed image. As an alternative
approach to the evaluation of reader image quality, Hawken
(1975) includes a packet of specially-prepared microfiche
consisting of: 1) an overall pattern of finely spaced small
dots of uniform size which can be used to assess the
sharpness and evenness of a screen image from center to edges
and corners; and 2) test pages exhibiting very finely detailed
typographic characterisitcs. The accompanying handbook contains
the test pages printed at eye-legible size. By comparing the
displayed microimages with the printed test pages, librarians
will be able to make fairly reliable judgments about the optical
performance of a reader. Because of quality controls inherent
in the COM recording process, the display of upper-case alphanumeric

116

COM reports generally requires reader resolution well below
that needed for readers used to display of microfilmed newspaper
pages and similar source documents.

As applied to readers, contrast denotes the relationship
between light and dark areas within displayed microimages.
All other reader specifications being equal, high contrast
screens are preferred for COM applications. Contrast is
affected by screen color -- the darker shades being of generally
higher contrast. Distortions are optical defects that, for
example, cause straight lines at screen edges to appear curved.
In low-priced readers, slight screen distortions are inevitable
but rarely significant in most library COM applications.
Distortion-free display is significant, however, in COM graphics
applications.

General Engineering

From the genral engineering standpoint, COM readers
selected for library applications must be designed for durability
and stability particularly if they are to be used by the public.
Durability assures the long-life that is essential to cost-savings
in applications involving the replacement of line printer output
with COM-generated microfilm or microfiche. Acceptable reader
case materials include steel, aluminum, and high-impact plastic.
The screen should be unbreakable or shatterproof. COM readers
intended for use in North American libraries should operate
from a standard 120 volt, sixty cycle AC outlet. Lamps and

other replaceable parts should be easily accessible and readily obtainable. The Micro Design 4010, a COM fiche reader, features an extendable modular drawer containing the optical assembly for simplified owner maintenance. Several COM readers -- the Kodak Ektalite series, for example -- utilize ordinary automotive lamps. Others use quartz-halogen bulbs which are much costlier but will operate for hundreds of hours before failure.

Because the vesicular and diazo microforms used in most COM applications may be damaged by excessive heat, the National Micrographics Association (1977) recommends that temperatures at the reader film gate not exceed seventy-five degrees centigrade (167 degrees farenheit). For user protection, metal case temperatures should not exceed fifty degrees centigrade (142 degrees farenheit). Plastic case temperatures should not exceed sixty degrees centigrade (152 degrees farenheit).

From the general engineering standpoint, the film transport is an important reader component requiring careful examination. The film transport is the mechanism that moves microimages past the reader lens. In reel microfilm, cartridge, and cassette readers, the transport may be manual or motorized, the latter moving film at about ten feet per second. Variable speed advance is an especially desirable film transport feature. Motorized cartridge film transports may provide for automatic threading onto a take-up spool as well. Being more complex than their manual counterparts, such automatic threading mechanisms may not prove consistently reliable. While motorized film transports

are obviously faster, manual transport systems are less vulnerable
to malfunction and may prove easier for the inexperienced user
to manipulate. Whether manual or motorized, the transport mechanism
should minimize film scratching.

Microfiche readers employ a carrier assembly that holds
the fiche between two pieces of flat glass. The carrier operates
on a slide and must move freely in both horizontal and vertical
directions, but not so freely as to drift. Most available COM
readers employ manual transport mechanisms. For applications
requiring rapid retrieval from large fiche files, Image Systems
and the Bruning Division of Addressograph-Multigraph offer
microfiche readers that automatically display designated images
on instructions entered at an operator keyboard. Image Systems'
Mentor retrieval device, for example, has capacity for 780 fiche
containing a total of 182,520 at a 48:1 reduction ration. Such
display devices are priced from $5,000 to $10,000 and are difficult
to cost-justify in most library COM applications.

Reader Size

Most COM microfiche readers are designed for deak-top operation
and occupy the area of an office typewriter. Readers for reel
microfilm, cartridges, and cassettes tend to be slightly
larger than microfiche equipment, although compact models are
available. The 3M 702 Cartridge Reader, for example, measures
just nineteen inches wide by twenty-four inches deep.

The desk-top COM reader is portable only in the sense of being light enough to be carried easily. Several microfiche readers are available for applications requiring portability. Such readers generally weigh four to seven pounds and are about the size of a large reference book. From the engineering standpoint, portable readers must be well-built to withstand abuses in transport and use and should have a strong, convenient handle.

Microforms Accepted and Magnification

Most COM readers are single-purpose devices designed to accept either 105mm by 148mm microfiche or 16mm microfilm on reels, in cartridges, or in cassettes. Cartridge and cassette readers, as noted above, will accept only the cartridges or cassettes of designated suppliers. Most COM fiche readers will also accept microfilm jackets and, when equipped with a tab-sized carrier, aperture cards.

While a given COM reader may physically accept a particular microform, the magnification may be inappropriate. Magnification is a statement of the ratio of a given linear dimension of a displayed microimage to the corresponding linear dimension of the microimage itself. The magnification ratio is expressed as 1:24, 1:42, 1:48, and so on, where the displayed microimage is enlarged twenty-four, forty-two, or forty-eight times.

The reader magnification must be appropriate to the effective reduction at which the COM images to be displayed were recorded.

A COM image recorded at an effective reduction of 42:1 will be read at full-size when magnified 1:42. Full-size magnification is, however, rarely required in COM applications. Being designed for legibility, COM images can often be usefully displayed at about three quarters of original size -- an image recorded at an effective reduction of 42:1, for example, would be magnified only 1:32. Readers employing three-quarter magnification are generally compact and require less desk-space than their full-size counterparts. The 3M Consort, a three-quarter size fiche reader, occupies only twelve by fifteen inches of desk surface. At the other extreme, COM-generated library catalogs and other reports containing small type faces or detailed graphics can be over-magnified -- a 1:50 enlargement of a 42:1 microimage, for example -- to facilitate viewing. Schleifer and Adams (1976) report that, in an experiment with a COM-generated edition of Books in Print at the Lehman College Library, staff members cited the ability to overmagnify small type sizes as an important advantage that minimized eye fatigue and facilitated acceptance. The producers of MARCFICHE, the COM-generated bibliographic product discussed in Section One, likewise recommend overmagnification for ease of use.

Given the widespread availability of COM-generated microforms at the three effective reductions of 24:1, 42:1, and 48:1, the fixed-lens, single-magnification reader is an obvious deterrent to systems development and change. Readers with interchangeable lenses are more flexible and represent a much better investment, especially in smaller libraries with very limited equipment budgets. Such readers accomplish magnification changes in several ways, depending on the model. The WSI Mini Cat microfiche reader, for example, offers the user a choice of two track-mounted lenses in the range 1:12 to 1:48. Several other manufacturers employ turret- or track-mounted, dual- or triple-magnification lens systems. This captive lens approach to magnification change is preferred for two reasons: 1) focus is maintained as the magnification is changed; and 2) captive lenses cannot easily be stolen. Several readers employ drop-in lenses which, because they are designed to be quickly and conveniently removed, are vulnerable to theft in public-use applications.

Screen-Size and Orientation

Regardless of magnification, the amount of information that can be displayed at any one time is limited by the reader's screen size and orientation. Full-size COM reader screens measure approximately eleven by fourteen inches. Three-quarter size reader screens measure approximately eight by eleven inches. In both cases, the long dimension of the screen is horizontal to accommodate the computer printout page-images normally employed in COM recording. For applications employing eighty or fewer characters per recorded line, however, the source document screen orientation, in which the long dimension is vertical, is preferred.

For library catalogs and similar applications oriented toward lines rather than pages of information, the NCR model 4600-11 fiche reader features a short (2.6 high by 12.5 inch wide) screen designed to display about twenty lines of data at eighty-seven percent of original size. The reader itself measures 12.8 by 13.1 inches at its base and is only 11.8 inches high.

Special Display Features

Image rotation is a special display feature that enables the user to turn displayed microimages to compensate for the varying positions of documents on film. As discussed in Section Two, most COM recorders will orient 16mm roll microfilm images in either the cine or the comic mode. While the two filming modes are normally not intermixed on the same COM-generated microform, image rotation can be a desirable, and perhaps essential, display feature for libraries acquiring COM-generated roll microforms from more than one source. A minimum ninety degree rotation is required to turn improperly-oriented images to the correct position for reading. Image rotation is not essential with COM fiche readers, since COM standard microfiche formats prescribe comic mode recording.

To minimize microform handling and facilitate retrieval, several COM microfiche readers employ a double carrier that will accept two fiche simultaneously. This special feature is extremely valuable in public-use COM applications where, for example, a 500 page catalog is recorded on two 48:1 fiche and maintained in the dual carrier, thereby eliminating the possibility that a user will have to change fiche to view a particular section of the catalog. Some readers have a larger carrier capable of accepting up to four fiche at once.

Human Factors in Reader Selection

Human factors is an interdisciplinary field that recognizes and emphasizes those elements that influence the effectiveness with which people can utilize equipment to accomplish its intended purpose. Meister (1971) provides an excellent introduction to human factors theory and practice. In a departure from their historic emphasis on technological innovation, micrographics equipment manufacturers are becoming increasingly aware of the importance of human factors analysis in facilitating user acceptance of microforms as a viable information communication medium. The application of human factors principles to reader design is discussed in a recent article by Landau (1977) which includes a bibliography.

Kottenstette and associates (1969,1970,1971), in a series of experiments at the Denver Research Institute, found that users responded negatively to certain perceived discrepancies between the retrieval of information from microforms and the retrieval of comparable information from paper documents. The user must often work very hard to accommodate himself to these discrepancies. In cases where the information need is not

sufficiently pressing, microform use may be discontinued. The
reader selected for library COM applications should minimize
perceived discrepancies between microform and hard-copy
presentations while reducing the level of accommodation required
for microform use.

Kottenstette (1971) identified difficulties in maintaining
focus and uneven screen illumination as serious reader defects
which may cause the user to abandon a microform presentation.
The user of a COM library catalog, for example, must be able
to easily establish focus and maintain it from frame to frame,
just as he or she does in turning the pages of a paper-edition
book catalog or in flipping through trays of cards. Uniform
screen illumination is important to user comfort. Even very
small areas of obviously greater brightness are undesirable.
Because its light source is above the viewing surface, the
front projection COM reader typically provides fairly uniform
screen illumination. Many newer rear projection readers, however,
feature high gain screens with a powerful light source that
appears much brighter at screen center. The resulting displayed
images are well-suited to ambient light viewing but may be somewhat
darker at the screen corners and contain "hot spots," deficiencies
of diffusion manifested in a halo effect. The best rear projection
COM readers employ screens that are carefully coated to diffuse
light. But high gain screens may not be viewable at wide angles --
that is, from positions other than directly in front of the

reader. This may prove a disadvantage in library technical services applications where, for example, a cataloger, with worksheets spread out in the center of a desk, must refer to COM-generated bibliographic data in a reader located to the right or left of the direct line of vision.

The noise of the fan that dissipates reader heat may be a significant irritant to many COM users. The National Micrographics Association (1977) recommends that reader noise levels not exceed sixty decibels above the threshold of hearing. Several newer readers -- the Kodak Ektalite series, for example -- dissipate heat by natural convection and, having no fan, are completely silent.

Reader design must recognize the complex inter-relationship between work surface and screen display. Front projection readers, with viewing surfaces approximately at table-top level, preserve the customary spatial relationship between note pad and material displayed, permitting both to be held in the same field of vision. Kottenstette (1971) found that persons wearing eyeglasses or contact lenses in an experiment involving the prolonged use of rear-projection readers could not comfortably glance from screen to note pad since, in most cases, the full value of lens correction could not be obtained without tipping the head when looking at the upright screen. Such students lost their place easily and could not successfully integrate the several tasks involved in microform use. Rear projection readers are available with screens that are slightly tilted away from the users. Users of the GAF 7700 can adjust the screen angle to personal preference. In a study of the impact of screen angle on microform reading, however, Lee and Buck (1975) found that, while users expressed a strong preference for tilted screens, their actual reading performance, measured in fewer eye fixations and regressions, definitely improved with a vertical screen. Over and above this finding, the study underscores the importance of subjective preference in acceptance or rejection of microform readers.

User Instruction

The need for user instruction is common to all equipment-dependent systems. In commercial applications and some special libraries, COM users constitute a closed group and can, consequently, be trained by co-workers or equipment vendors. In the case of COM catalogs and similar reports generated by public and academic libraries, however, microform readers will be available to a broad user group, many of whom neither ask for, nor receive, instruction. Potential problems arising from this situation can be minimized, but not entirely eliminated, by placing step-by-step instructions, with diagrams, near the reader. Several newer readers have operating instructions permanently displayed on the reader case. As Spaulding (1977) notes, such printed instructions are most effective when accompanied by a personal demonstration that explains the reader's operating features.

Operating controls should be clearly labelled. Controls should be readily accessible by both right- and left-handed persons. Reader operation should be predictable. When the film advance knob is turned clockwise, for example, the film should move forward.

Cost

Table 3, presented earlier in this Section, indicated the high cost of roll microform readers compared to fiche readers of comparable quality. Prices for high-quality, desk-top COM fiche readers range from approximately two hundred dollars to four hundred dollars. The more expensive models generally feature larger screens, several lenses, and dual- or tab-size fiche carriers. The less expensive COM fiche readers offer these features as extra cost options, if at all. Prices for portable COM fiche readers begin at around 125 dollars. Sizeable quantity purchases will generally lower individual reader prices by ten to twenty percent. Public and academic libraries may be eligible for additional discounts offered to government agencies and other non-profit institutions.

Prices for 16mm reel microfilm readers begin at around four hundred dollars and peak at around one thousand dollars. Again, higher-priced models include such features as larger screens, interchangeable magnifications, image rotation, and motorized film advance. Prices for self-threading cartridge and cassette readers range between seven hundred and two thousand dollars. The selection of such devices is, however, limited since manufacturers of cartridge and cassette equipment have traditionally emphasized reader/printers rather than readers.

In COM applications involving the replacement of line printer output, the number of required readers is generally equal to the number of previously-produced paper copies. Unfortunately, no adequate guidelines have been developed to determine the number of readers required to replace a card-form catalog.

Reader/Printers

A reader/printer, as the name implies, combines the function of a reader with the ability to make enlarged paper prints of displayed microimages. Reader/printer evaluation generally employs the criteria applicable to microform readers plus consideration of the acceptability of the printing process. For COM applications, the two most widely used printing technologies are the dry silver process and the electrofax process.

Dry silver microfilms were described in Section Two in connection with the 3M EBR and LBR COM recorders. 3M dry silver reader/printers employ a specially-treated paper which, after exposure, is developed by heat, without additional chemicals. The dry silver process is clean and convenient. Letter-size prints are delivered in approximately ten seconds. Print quality is acceptable for most applications, but developed prints retain light sensitivity and are subject to fading. Print permanence is, however, rarely a user requirement in most library COM applications. The dry silver process is polarity-reversing. Negative microforms are required to make positive prints.

The electrofax process is a variant of the electrostatic technology that currently dominates the office copier industry. Light transmitted through a microimage and lens forms a latent enlargement on charged photoreceptive paper coated with zinc oxide in a resin binder. The latent image is developed through the application of an oppositely-charged toner, consisting of fine carbon particles in liquid suspension. Developed prints are delivered dry and are as permanent as the paper on which they are made. Print time is approximately ten to fifteen seconds. Print quality is acceptable for most library COM applications. Although the electrofax process is normally polarity-maintaining, most electrofax reader/printers incorporate a switch that permits the user to make positive-appearing prints from either positive or negative microimages. Electrofax reader/printer manufacturers include Bell and Howell, Kodak, MISI, and Oce Industries.

Prices for dry silver and electrofax reader/printers are comparable. Microfiche models cost upwards of one thousand dollars, with roll microform equipment prices beginning at 2,500 dollars. When supplies are ordered in sufficient quantities, the cost per print approaches five cents.

<u>The Surrounding Environment</u>

In terms of use patterns, library COM applications can be divided into two broad groups: reference-type and study-type. The distinction is well-described by Kottenstette (1969,1970, 1971) within the general context of microform use. Reference-type applications -- typified by COM-generated library catalogs and circulation lists -- involve the brief scanning of displayed COM images to retrieve small amounts of information which serve as the basis for action. The microform catalog user, for example, finds the desired entry, usually within an alphabetic arrangement on film or fiche; determines the item location from the class number of other indicator; then enters the stack area to obtain the item. Transaction and machine contact time are typically brief. DeBruin (1977) reports that less than thirty percent of COM catalog users at the University of Toronto Library spent more than five minutes per incident in author, title, or call number searches. Given an adequate reader, user resistance tends to be low, even among those persons who have had previously unfavorable experiences with microforms. In a survey of COM catalog users at the Georgia Tech library, for example, Greene (1975) found no correlation between attitude toward microforms and frequency of COM use in a reference-type application.

In study-type applications, COM-generated microforms are read or otherwise intensively examined for their substantive content. Many of the COM-generated bibliographic products and micropublications described in Section One fall into this group. Unlike the brief reference-type transactions described above, the use of microforms in study is a complex activity involving cognition, reflection, and prolonged machine contact. A cataloger, for example, may refer to MARCFICHE or the COM edition of Library of Congress Subject Headings, Eighth Edition many times throughout a work day. Close examination of entries may be required. In the design of such applications, careful attention must be given to the integration of the reader into the work environment.

Lighting has a significant impact on efficient performance in difficult visual tasks, including microform use. Holmes (1970) recommends that microform use areas be designed with indirect and reflected lighting of fifteen to twenty foot-candles at the work surface. Experiments by Lee and Buck (1975), however, indicate that work performance remains insensitive to ambient light variations in the range ten to thirty foot-candles.

Retrieval Coding and Indexing

The success of many microform applications depends on the ability to rapidly locate one or more specified microimages

from among hundreds or thousands. Microform indexing and
retrieval systems have been well described by Courtot (1975).
COM recording is compatible with a wide range of retrieval
coding and indexing techniques for both roll microforms and
micorfiche.

Eye-Legible Characters for Roll Microforms

In source document applications, one of the simplest
retrieval techniques for roll microforms utilizes flash targets
with blank frames to separate groups of related microimages.
These flash targets function like file folder tabs or dividers,
directing the user to the area in which the relevant microimage
is located but not to the microimage itself. The technique is
sometimes supported by sequential document or frame numbering.
Like source document cameras, most COM recorders will create
frames containing eye-legible alphanumeric characters. These
frames can precede groups of conventional microimages or appear
beneath all or selected frames on a roll of film. The COM-generated
eye-legible characters generally indicate groups of related
microimages arranged in numeric or alphabetic sequence.
Alternatively, they may represent sequential frame numbers or
be extracted, through software, from the data itself in order
to display, for example, the first and last entries on a given
frame. At retrieval time, eye-legible targets catch the user's
eye as the film advances rapidly.

Odometer Indexing

Odometer indexing is an effective roll film retrieval technique in which the location of a microimage is a function of its distance from the beginning of the roll. In source document applications, the index is prepared manually by examining processed microimages on a reader or reader/printer equipped with an odometer and then associating the desired retrieval parameters with their odometer readings. In COM applications, computer software can be used to derive odometer readings prior to the actual recording of images on film. The odometer index can then be recorded as the first microimage on the roll to which it pertains. The index may also be typed on labels affixed to roll film containers or cartridges, maintained in a card file, printed, or stored in machine-readable form for computer inquiry. At retrieval time, the index is consulted to determine the desired odometer reading. The user mounts the proper roll or cartridge on the reader and, while watching the odometer, advances the film to the appropriate point. Proximity of the desired microimage to the indicated odometer reading depends on specificity of indexing but is, in most cases, approximate.

In a variant of odometer indexing, the ROM 3 COM Terminal and LTR 1100 -- the two readers designed specifically for use with library COM catalogs -- feature a side-mounted scale corresponding to the film footage position of alphabetic groupings on film (fig. 28). The user, watching the scale, advances the

Figure 28
ROM 3 Microform Viewer Showing Side-Mounted Index Strip
(Courtesy: Brodart)

film to the desired alphabetic grouping and then proceeds
slowly to locate desired entries.

Image Count Marks (Blips)

An image count mark, or blip, is an opaque rectangular
mark that appears beneath each microimage on 16mm roll microfilm
(fig. 29). A form slide is typically used to position the image
count mark on COM-generated microfilm. At retrieval time, a
Recordak Microstar, 3M Page Search, COR 701EC, or equivalent
reader or reader/printer equipped with a motorized film advance
and appropriate logical circuitry, will search by counting the
marks and stopping the film at the frame corresponding to the
number entered at an operator keyboard. The technique is, thus,
a variant of sequential frame numbering. The blips occupy the
same position from frame to frame and have no intrinsic information
content. An external index is used to determine the desired
image count number. The technique is especially useful for
high-speed, reliable microimage location in systems utilizing
computerized indexes that deliver a roll and frame number address
within a microfilm data base. Basic principles of such systems
are discussed by Teplitz (1971). The 3M Microdisc, described
by Shepard (1975), is one of several available retrieval systems
that combine computer-based index maintenance with 16mm microfilm
encoded with image count marks.

Code-Lines

Code-line indexing -- developed by Eastman Kodak under the
trade-name Kodaline -- utilizes a series of short, graduated

Figure 29
Image Count Marks

bars between microimages on 16mm roll microfilm (fig. 30). The

vertical placement of the lines denotes numeric information

such as a sequential frame number, an account number, or a

numerically-encoded subject descriptor. The Kodak KOM-80 and

KOM-85 recorders utilize software to place the code-lines on

film. The code-line positions are assigned sequentially. The

numbers to be represented may be derived from the data itself.

At retrieval time, an external index is consulted to determine

the desired code-line position. When the film is advanced at

high speed in a motorized reader, the microimages are blurred

and the code-lines appear continuous. A scale alongside the

reader screen indicates the code value of each line position.

Inclusion of code-lines requires a slight increase in the amount

of space between frames, thereby descreasing the microimage

capacity of a roll by five to ten percent.

MIRAcode and Oracle Coding

MIRAcode is the trade name for a group of Eastman Kodak

products that provide subject or other access to microimages

within 16mm cartridges. The name itself is derived from a

photo-optical binary code which appears on film as columns

of clear and opaque bits, perpendicular to the film edge and

adjacent or their corresponding microimages (fig. 31). Each column

uses twelve bit positions to represent three digits in the Excess-3

code. A special MIRAcode Retrieval Terminal contains the logic

and motor controls required to advance the film, interpret the

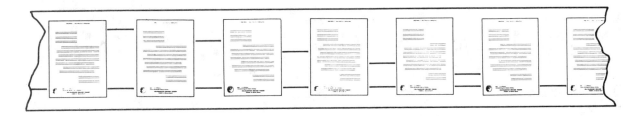

Figure 30
Code-Line Indexing

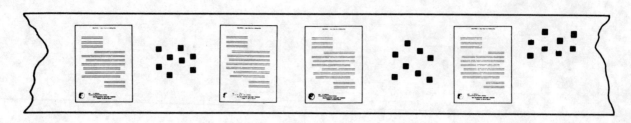

Figure 31
MIRAcode

140

code, and stop the film at relevant microimages in response to search statements of verying complexity. The best introduction to the system's various components is by Wilcox (1973). Its applicability to library retrieval problems has been discussed by Janda (1968), Janda and Gordon (1970), and Fournier and Schoenfeld (1973).

In source document applications of MIRAcode, a 16mm planetary camera equipped with a keyboard is used to record microimages and numeric code. For COM applications, the Kodak KOM-80, Beta COM 700H, Cal Comp 1675, Applicon AP75, and other recorders offer optional MIRAcode capability. Some COM recorders -- the Kodak KOM-80, for example -- place the MIRAcode bits _after_ the relevant microimage on film. Since source document MIRAcode cameras place the code _before_ the relevant microimage, modification of the MIRAcode Retrieval Terminal is required for successful retrieval on equipment originally set up for source document microfilm. COM systems designers should also be aware that the preparation of coding information prior to filming can be time-consuming and the addition of code columns to film will significantly reduce recording speed. The code columns themselves occupy space on film, thereby significantly diminishing the microimage capacity of individual rolls.

For applications which do not require the full power of MIRAcode, Kodak recently introduced a lower-priced retrieval system that provides access to randomly-filmed microimages through an eight-digit binary code located beneath each 16mm microimage. The system, called <u>Oracle</u>, includes a planetary source document microfilmer with key-to-film encoder and a special retrieval terminal. Oracle-coded 16mm microfilm can also be generated by the Kodak KOM-85 recorder.

Eye-Legible Microfiche Titling

The retrieval of catalog entries or other information stored on microfiche requires location of both the appropriate fiche and the desired frame within the fiche. In manual systems, location of the appropriate fiche is facilitated by eye-legible titling. Each microfiche typically reserves the first row of frames for such titling. All COM recorders capable of producing microfiche will record eye-legible characters in the title area. The most versatile COM recorders -- the DatagraphiX 4500 Series or Cal Comp 2100, for example -- will generate one, two, or three lines of appropriately-sized titling. In some cases, different sizes of eye-legible characters can be mixed within the title area (fig. 32). While the title area normally appears at the top of the fiche, the Bell and Howell 3700 will position eye-legible characters along the bottom row of frames or in either end column. Some COM recorders permit the title area to be of reverse polarity to further highlight it.

Depending on the capabilities of recorder hardware and software, information for the title area may be captured in

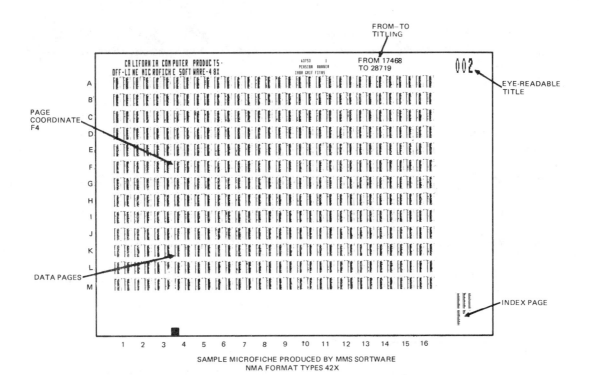

SAMPLE MICROFICHE PRODUCED BY MMS SORTWARE
NMA FORMAT TYPES 42X

Figure 32
Microfiche Titling and Indexing
(Courtesy: California Computer Products, Inc.)

several ways. With the Cal Comp Microfiche Management System,
for example, title information may be entered directly by the
COM operator at run-time, derived from one or more fields in
the data being recorded, or calculated by the application
program. Most eye-legible microfiche titling contains a mix
of: 1) user-supplied fixed information, such as a report name;
and 2) software-derived variable information, such as fiche
sequence number, date, and inclusive fiche contents, typically
expressed as a "from-to" statement of index keys extracted
from the first and last data frames.

For applications with very heavy reference activity, COM
software can generate a few additional eye-legible characters
at the top of each column of frames. These eye-legible column
headings speed retrieval by narrowing the search to particular
areas on fiche.

Microfiche Indexing

Information from alphabetically-arranged library catalogs,
call number lists of items in circulation, and other sequentially-
ordered microfiche reports can often be retrieved successfully
without indexing. Many COM applications, however, require an
index to associate desired data with its location in a particular
microfiche frame. The most prevalent COM microfiche formats
provide for an index as the last frame on a fiche, positioned
in the lower right hand corner. Placement of the index frame
in this position is essential in applications anticipating the

use of automatic fiche retrieval and display equipment such as the Bruning Model 95 or Image Systems' CARD reader. As with microfiche titling, software is utilized to extract class numbers, authors, titles, or other user-specified index keys from each data frame and list them in the index with their associated microfiche grid coordinates, expressed as an alphabetic row designator and numeric column designator. The ease with which this is accomplished varies with the software package. Cal Comp's Microfiche Management System, for example, permits extraction of index data regardless of its specific location on a page. Vendor-supplied indexing packages, while very versatile, are written for the straightforward applications encountered in most report production environments. As noted in Section Two, special indexing requirements must be programmed by the user.

If more than one index frame is required, they customarily occupy the last few corner frames. The best COM software automatically provides for a variable number of index frames. Instead of, or in addition to, the corner index, there is an increasing trend toward the placement of index frames at the top of each fiche column. These column indexes may be identical with, or more detailed versions of, the corner index. The column index technique sacrifices a few data frames to facilitate retrieval by keeping the user in close proximity to an index.

Another increasingly popular technique provides for a randomly-recorded microfiche or microfilm data base -- of catalog entries, for example -- controlled by a master index on one or more separate fiche. Each index entry delivers a roll number and frame number or a fiche number and grid coordinates. If both the data base and index are on fiche, a dual carrier reader can be used to facilitate rapid referral from one microform to the other. For data bases on 16mm microfilm with a fiche index, the COR 701 reader will accept a cartridge and a fiche simultaneously. The microfiche master index technique, with a non-cumulating microfiche data base of catalog entries, is used by MARCFICHE.

SECTION FIVE

LINKS TO OTHER SYSTEMS

In addition to functioning as a viable alternative to
line printers and on-line information systems, COM can interface
with equipment for the economical production of paper reports.
In addition, the development of computer-input-microfilm (CIM)
technology offers potential for extending a wide range of data
processing capabilities to COM-recorded information.

Printing/Publishing

Several options are available for libraries requiring
multiple-copy full-size paper output from microform data bases.
The DatagraphiX 7000 Microfilm Input Platemaker will project
enlarged COM microimages onto nine by twelve inch Datalith
silver emulsion plates suitable for off-set printing of up to
five thousand copies. The DatagraphiX 7000 accepts 16mm or 35mm
roll microfilm, in either cine or comic mode. Magnification
ranges from 3X to 36X. The Information International 800
Projection Platemaker produces off-set masters from 16mm or
35mm microfilm in sizes ranging from 8.5 by 11 to 12 by 18
inches. The 800 automatically searches for specified frames
using image count marks. The LogE COM Printer automatically
makes electrostatic offset plates or paper copies from 35mm
microfilm at enlargements of 7X to 20X. Maximum print size is
twelve by eighteen inches. For COM applications requiring a few
paper copies for annotation or other reasons, the Xerox 970 is

a programmable enlarger/printer capable of producing single
or multiple plain-paper copies from all or selected microimages
on standard microfiche in several formst. Use of the Xerox 970
in COM applications is discussed by Greenwold (1976).

Computer-Input-Microfilm

Computer-input-microfilm (CIM) is a variant of optical
character recognition. A CIM device scans, interprets, and
translates human-readable information on microfilm to machine-
readable digital data on magnetic tape or other media. Thus,
CIM is conceptually the opposite of COM. The advantages of CIM,
outlined by Harris (1977), are obvious. Tape, disk, and drum
storage are expensive, bulky, and vulnerable to deterioration
over time. Microfilm is economical, compact, and, when properly
processed, archivally stable. Information on microfilm offers
the additional advantage of being human-readable, permitting the
simultaneous creation of reports for reading and computer re-entry.

Although CIM technology is still developing, the advantages
of microfilm over paper in optical character recognition systems
have long been recognized. Compact microfilm is easier to
handle than bulky paper. Input documents need not be of uniform
size. The paper jams commonly experienced with high-speed
paper-document feeders are eliminated. Microfilm character
recognition is accomplished by transmitted light rather than
the more powerful reflected light required in paper OCR systems.
FOSDIC, one of the earliest CIM devices, has been used, in

several versions, since 1953 at the United States Census Bureau. Its application is described by Volk (1969) and McPherson and Volk (1962).

Grafix I, a complex and powerful CIM system developed by Information International, represents the state-of-the-art today. System descriptions are presented by Fenaughty (1974), Griffith (1975), and Holland (1976). Using a unique combination of hardware and software, Grafix I will read microfilmed source documents or COM microimages created in a variety of fonts and formats, including hand printing. Character recognition is accomplished through a masking technique enhanced by a probability algorithm. Broken type faces and hand printing are recognized by feature extraction. Rejected characters are displayed, with context, at an operator terminal for key-entered correction. Although any 35mm microfilm input can be accepted, best results are obviously obtained from high-quality COM microimages prepared by graphic recorders such as the Information International FR-80.

The first Grafix I was built for the United States Navy. The system has since been used in several library-related applications. For the DATUM Information Retrieval System, an automated legal data base developed at the University of Montreal, Grafix I converted 16,000 bi-lingual pages of printed Exchequer Court proceedings to machine-readable form. At the University of California at Irvine, the system has been used to encode Greek

text. In an application described by Burford and Clark (1975),
the Hydrologic Data Laboratory at the Agricultural Research
Service in Beltsville, Maryland uses Grafix I for computer
re-entry of data previously recorded on COM. A data-entry
error rate of less than one percent is reported.

As might be expected, Grafix I is a multi-million dollar
device. The currently high cost of CIM technology necessarily
limits its application in library work.

References

Anderson, Barbara J. (1973). "COM Restores Calm to the Los Angeles Public Library," Information and Records Management 7/5: 40-42.

Ardern, L.L. (1971). "COM, PCMI, and Books in English," Microdoc 10: 17-21.

Aschenborn, Hans J. (1972). "The Use of Microfilm in South African Libraries," Journal of Micrographics 6: 33-37.

Avedon, Don (1976). The User's Guide to Standard Microfiche Formats (Silver Spring: National Micrographics Association).

Avedon, Don M. (1969). "Computer Output Microfilm: an NMA Survey of the Field," Journal of Micrographics 3: 7-12.

Barrett, W.J. (1972). "The Evaluation of Microfilm Readers," Journal of Micrographics 6: 51-63.

Bernstein, George B. (1972). "Why 24X/48X?," Journal of Micrographics 5: 295-300.

Bolef, Doris (1974). "Computer-Output-Microfilm," Special Libraries 65: 169-75.

Bolnick, Franklin I. (1971). "On-Line Versus Off-Line COM Systems," Journal of Micrographics 4: 123-31.

Boyd, Sherman H. (1973). "Technology of Computer Output Microfilm: Past, Present and Future," TAPPI 56: 107-10.

Buckle, David (1974). "The Cost of a COM Catalogue System at Birmingham University Library," Microdoc 13: 15-18.

Buckle, David and French, Thomas (1971). "The Application of Microform to Manual and Machine-Readable Catalogues," Program 5: 41-6.

Burford, J.B. and Clark, J.M. (1975). "Hydrologic Data -- Computer-Microfilm Storage and Retrieval," Journal of Micrographics 8: 147-51.

Courtot, Marilyn (1975). Microform Indexing and Retrieval Systems (Silver Spring: National Micrographics Association).

DeBruin, Valentine (1977). "Sometimes Dirty Things are Seen on the Screen: a Mini-Evaluation of the COM Microcatalogue at the University of Toronto Library," Journal of Academic Librarianship 3: 256-66.

Doran, Thomas G. (1971). "Micrographic Reports: a New Dimension for Management," Journal of Micrographics 4: 133-41.

Enders, Dick (1975). "COM Viewers -- a Generalized Overview of their History, Growth, and Future Direction," Proceedings of the National Microfilm Association 24: 165-69.

Fenaughty, Alfred L. (1975). "Demand Printing: a Revolution in Publishing," Journal of Micrographics 8: 201-206.

Firisen, J.M. (1971). "Series F Electron Beam Recording System," Microdoc 10: 45-9.

Fischer, Mary L. (1973). "The Use of COM at the Los Angeles Public Library," Journal of Micrographics 6: 205-10.

Forbes, Edward J. and Bagg, Thomas C. (1966). Report of a Study of Requirements and Specifications for Serial and Monograph Microrecording for the National Library of Medicine (Washington, D.C.: National Bureau of Standards).

Fournier, Jacques and Schoenfeld, Alison (1973). "The Development of an Electronic Film Retrieval System for a Newspaper Library," Proceedings of the American Society for Information Science 10: 67-9.

Greene, Robert J. (1975). "Microform Attitude and Frequency of Microform Use," Journal of Micrographics 8: 131-4.

Greene, Robert J. (1975a). "Microform Library Catalogs and the LENDS Microfiche Catalog," Microform Review 4: 30-34.

Greenwold, Douglas J. (1976). "Rethinking 24X COM from a New Perspective," Journal of Micrographics 10: 55-6.

Griffith, Arnold K. (1975). "From Gutenberg to Frafix I -- New Directions in OCR," Journal of Micrographics 9: 81-9.

Grosso, P.F. and Tarnowski, A.A. (1976). "Electron Beam Recording on Film -- Applications and Performance," Electro-Optical Systems Design 8: 57-61.

Harris, Barry (1977). "Practical Considerations of the COM/CIM Marriage," Information Hotline 9: 6-9.

Harrison, Tom L. (1973). "CRT vs. COM -- Real Time vs. Real Time Enough," Journal of Micrographics 7: 37-44.

Harrison, Tom L. (1974). "COM: the Information Form that Fits the EDP Environment," Journal of Micrographics 7: 199-203.

Hawken, William R. (1975). _Evaluating Microfiche Readers: a Handbook for Librarians_ (Washington: Council on Library Resources).

Hawken, William R. (1968). "Microform Standardization: the Problem of Research Materials and a Proposed Solution," _NMA Journal_ 2: 14-27.

Heacock, James F. (1975). "The Evolution and New Developments in Films for the Micrographics Industry," _Proceedings of the National Microfilm Association_ 24: 73-5.

Herbert, P.H. (1971). "A New Concept in COM Printers," _Microdoc_ 10: 66-71.

Hirschsohn, Ian (1977). "Case Studies of the Dramatic Rise of COM Graphics," _Proceedings of the National Micrographics Association_ 26: 3-6.

Holland, Roger (1976). "CIM -- the Present and the Future," _Microdoc_ 15: 52-55.

Holmes, Donald C. (1970). _Determination of the Environmental Conditions Required in a Library for the Effective Utilization of Microforms_ (Washington: Office of Education, Bureau of Research).

Horst, Robert P. (1974). "COM in Business Graphics: a Better Way to Present Management Reports," _Proceedings of the National Microfilm Association_ 23: II-96-9.

Jacob, Mary E. (1975). "More with Less: New Technical Services Developments in the University of Sydney Library," _Australian Library Journal_ 24: 388-9.

Janda, Kenneth (1968). "Political Research with Miracode: a 16mm Microfilm Information Retrieval System," _NMA Journal_ 1: 41-47.

Janda, Kenneth and Gordon, David (1970). "A Microfilm Information Retrieval System for Newspaper Libraries," _Special Libraries_ 61: 33-47.

Judisch, J.M. (1968). "The Effect of Positive-Negative Microforms and Front-Rear Projection on Reading Speed and Comprehension," _NMA Journal_ 2: 58-61.

Kottenstette, James (1969). _An Investigation of the Characteristics of Ultrafiche and its Application to Colleges and Universities_ (Washington, D.C.: Office of Education, Bureau of Research).

Kottenstette, James (1970). "User Behavior: Requirements," in <u>Microform Utilization: the Academic Library Environment</u> (Denver: University of Denver), pp. 158-166.

Kottenstette, James (1971). "Testing Student Reactions to Educational Microforms: Many Problems - a Few Answers," <u>Journal of Micrographics</u> 4: 73-78 (1971).

Kottenstette, James and Dailey, K. Anne (1971). <u>An Investigation of the Environment for Educational Microform Use</u> (Denver: Denver Research Institue).

Kozumplik, W.A. and Lange, R.T. (1967). "Computer-Produced Microfilm Library Catalog," <u>American Documentation</u> 18: 67-80.

Kurttila, Kenneth R. (1977). "Dry Silver Film Stability," <u>Journal of Micrographics</u> 10: 113-119.

LaHood, Charles G., Jr. (1977). "Selecting and Evaluating Microform Reading Equipment for Libraries," <u>Microform Review</u> 6: 79.

Lamar, J.V. and Stratton, R.H. (1974). "Digital Weather Data Displayed in a Colored Image Format," <u>Journal of Micrographics</u> 7: 271-8.

Landau, Robert M. (1977). "Microfiche Reader Human Factors," <u>Journal of Micrographics</u> 10: 219-27.

Lee, David R. and Buck, James R. (1975). "The Effect of Screen Angle and Luminance on Microform Reading," <u>Human Factors</u> 17: 461-9.

Library Technology Program (1973). "Microfilm Readers for Libraries," <u>Library Technology Reports</u> (Chicago: American Library Association).

Linford, J.E. (1972). "Books in English," <u>Microform Review</u> 1: 207-13.

Malabarba, Frank (1975). "Microfilm Information Systems (MIS): A Data Base Alternative," <u>Journal of Micrographics</u> 9: 3-11.

Malinconico, S. Michael (1976). "The Display Medium and the Price of the Message," <u>Library Journal</u> 101: 2144-50.

Malinconico, S. Michael (1977). "The Economics of Computer Output Media," in J.L. Divilbiss, <u>The Economics of Library Automation: Proceedings of the 1976 Clinic on Library Applications of Data Processing</u> (Urbana-Champaign: University of Illinois, Graduate School of Library Science), 145-62.

McGrath, William E. and Simon, Donald (1972). "Regional Numerical Union Catalog on Computer Output Microfiche," Journal of Library Automation 5: 217-29.

McGregor, H.H. (1975). "Vesicular Photography -- an Overview," Journal of Micrographics 9: 13-20.

McPherson, James L. and Volk, Masey (1962). "FOSDIC Microfilm Problems and their Solutions," Proceedings of the National Microfilm Association 11: 193-203.

Meister, David (1971). Human Factors: Theory and Practice (New York: Wiley Interscience).

Meyer, Richard W. and Knapp, John F. (1975). "COM Catalog Based on OCLC Records," Journal of Library Automation 8: 312-31.

Meyers, W.C. (1971). "Non-Silver-Halide Laser Micrographic Recording Systems and Applications," in Proceedings of the Third International Congress on Reprography (London: IPC Science and Technology Press, 1971), pp. 39-47.

National Microfilm Association (1974). How to Select a Microfilm Reader or Reader/Printer (Silver Spring: National Microfilm Association).

National Micrographics Association (1977). Standard Specifications for Microform Readers. Standards Committee Working Document (Silver Spring: National Micrographics Association).

National Micrographics Association (1976). Format and Coding Standards for Computer-Output-Microfilm (Silver Springs: National Micrographics Association).

Neary, Dennis R. (1976). "Computer/Micrographics Integration Requires Cross Training," Journal of Micrographics 9: 315-6.

Neary, Dennis R., Coyle, Terrence H., and Avedon, Don M. (1976). "The Integration of Microfilm and the Computer," AFIPS Conference Proceedings 45: 627-639.

Norcross, J.A. and Sampath, P.I. (1973). "Non-Silver Photographic Materials and Lasers in the Micrographic Industry," in Chenevert, Don, ed., Micrographics Science 1973: Winter Symposium (Washington, D.C.: Society of Photographic Scientists and Engineers).

Paur, Tom R. (1976). "Formslides: Information for the User," Journal of Micrographics 9: 161-3.

Peoples, Bobby R. (1972). "COM Software -- State of the Art," Proceedings of the National Microfilm Association 21: II-84-90.

Quantor Corporation (1975). Facts on Film. (Mountain View, California: Quantor Corporation).

Roberts, E.G. and Kennedy, J,P. (1973). "The Georgia Tech Library's Microfiche Catalog," Journal of Micrographics 6: 245-51.

Robinson, W.D. (1973). "Today's Marketplace -- a Guide to COM Development," in Chenevert, Don, ed., Micrographics Science 1973: Winter Symposium (Washington, D.C.: Society of Photographic Scientists and Engineers).

Rogers, Kenneth A. and Vogt, Earl C. (1973). "Cost Benefits of Computer Output Microfilm Library Catalogs," Proceedings of the American Society for Information Science 10: 199-200.

Ross, Joan (1976). "The Great Output Race: COM Joins the Winner's Circle," Journal of Micrographics 10: 11-15.

Saffady, William (1974). "A Computer-Output-Microfilm List of Serials for Patron Use," Journal of Library Automation 7: 263-6.

Shepard, Joseph W. (1973). "Dry Silver Films," Proceedings of the National Microfilm Association 22: II-237-40.

Shepard, Joseph W. (1975). "Retrieval Systems Considerations," Journal of Micrographics 8: 285-8.

Sherman, Alonzo (1972). "How to Select a Microfilm Reader or Reader/Printer," Information and Records Management 6/4: 62-4.

Schleifer, Harold B. and Adams, Peggy A. (1976). "Books in Print on Microfiche: a Pilot Test," Microform Review 5: 10-24.

Simmons, Peter (1975). "Library Automation at the University of British Columbia: a Ten Year Progress Report," in Spigai, Frances, ed., Information Roundup: Proceedings of the Fourth ASIS Mid-Year Meeting (Washington, D.C.: American Society for Information Science).

Spaulding, Carl (1977). "Teaching the Use of Microfilm Readers," Microform Review 6: 80-81.

Spaulding, Carl and Fair, Judy H. (1975). "Micrographics 1974," Library Resources and Technical Services 19: 206-25.

Spencer, J.R. (1973). An Appraisal of Computer-Output-Microfilm for Library Catalogues (Hatfield: National Reprographic Centre for documentation).

Spreitzer, Francis (1972). "Microfilm Cartridges and Cassettes," Library Technology Reports (Chicago: American Library Association).

Stecher, Elizabeth (1975). "RMIT COM Catalogue Study Results," Australian Library Journal 24: 384-8.

Teplitz, Arthur A. (1971). "Computer-Controlled Retrieval: a Primer," Journal of Micrographics 5: 35-40.

Titus, Arthur C. (1972). "On-Line Processing in a COM System," Proceedings of the National Microfilm Association 21: III-21-32.

Ungerleider, L. (1973). "A Study of COM Usability in the Technical Processing Area of the Yale University Library," Journal of Micrographics 7: 81-90.

Veaner, Allen B. (1974). "Institutional, Political, and Fiscal Factors in the Development of Library Automation, 1967-71," Journal of Library Automation 7: 5-26.

Volk, Masey (1969). "Automated Input for the 1970 Census," Journal of Micrographics 3: 57-62.

Wells, Richard A. (1972). "What is COM Business Graphics?," Proceedings of the National Microfilm Association 21: II-92-5.

Wieselman, Irving L. (1977). "Hard Copy Computer Output and its Future," AFIPS Conference Proceedings 46: 363-70.

Wilcox, Stephen (1973). "Kodak MIRAcode II Products: Concept and Applications," in Chenevert, Don, ed., Micrographics Science 1973: Winter Symposium (Washington, D.C.: Society of Photographic Scientists and Engineers), pp. 13-28.

Wright, Gordon (1970). "Effective Reader Design," in Microform Utilization: the Academic Library Environment (Denver: University of Denver), pp. 148-57.

APPENDIX A

A GENERAL FORMULA FOR DETERMINING MONTHLY COM COSTS

The following is a general formula for the determination of
the monthly cost of a COM application:

$$(T + (L \times C) + (D \times F)) \times U + \frac{(R \times N)}{A} + M$$

Where:

T = the cost of preparing a print-tape or appropriately-
formatted COM tape utilizing one of the methodologies
described in Section Two of this report;

L = report length, expressed as the number of frames on
film or fiche;

C = the cost per frame to create COM master film or fiche,
adjusted to reflect additional charges for incomplete
rolls or fiche, as in the examples given in Section
Three of this report;

D = the number of required duplicates, typically expressed
as the number of frames for roll microform applications
or the number of fiche;

F = the cost per frame for duplicate roll microforms or
the cost per duplicate fiche;

U = the update frequency, expressed as the number of times
the COM report will be produced per month;

R = the cost per reader or other display device;

N = the number of use points to which the COM report will
be distributed;

A = the amortization period for readers or other display
devices, expressed in number of months of useful life;
if monthly rental or lease charges are substituted
for R, division by the amortization period is omitted;

M = the monthly equipment maintenance allowance or cost
per month of maintenance contracts.

APPENDIX B

COM RECORDER SPECIFICATION SUMMARIES

The specification summaries that appear on the following pages briefly describe individual COM recorders, emphasizing hardware and software features of particular significance to libraries. Emphasis is placed on COM recorders currently in production. A few older recorders -- the Kodak KOM-90, for example -- are included because of their continued use by COM service bureaus and in-house data processing centers. The summaries are, for the most part, compiled from vendor literature and other published sources and do not reflect customized configurations or special options that may be available. Vendor addresses are included to facilitate the procurement of more detailed information.

BELL AND HOWELL 3700 and 3800

Vendor: Bell and Howell Business Equipment Group
          COM Products
          1451 Quail Street
          P.O. Box 1940
          Newport, Beach, California 92663

General Description: The Bell and Howell 3700 is a high-speed,
          off-line alphanumeric COM recorder capable of producing
          16mm roll microfilm and 105mm microfiche from
          appropriately-formatted magnetic tapes prepared by
          most general-purpose computers. The 3700 was originally
          developed by Peripheral Technology, Inc. and marketed
          by Pertec Business Systems as the Pertec 3700. Bell
          and Howell acquired manufacturing rights from Pertec
          in 1974. The Bell and Howell 3800 is a minicomputer-
          controlled version of the 3700.

Recording Method and Speed: CRT, using a seven by nine dot
          matrix; rated speed is 26,000 lines per minute;
          typical throughput is in the range 12,000 to
          19,000 lines per minute.

Input Requirements: seven or nine track, NRZ or PE tapes,
          recorded at 556, 800, or 1600 bits per inch; 6250
          bits per inch available as an option; EBCDIC, ASCII,
          and BCD codes standard; optional translators for the
          3700 will accept codes generated by UNIVAC 1108,
          Honeywell 200 and 6000, NCR Century and 315, GE 425/435,
          CDC 6400, and other computers.

Software Support: for 3700, callable subroutines and
          print-tape translator packages available; COMDATA
          report generator package permits creation of
          titled and indexed microfiche directly from raw
          data files; for 3800, PDP 11/04 utilized as
          pre-processor with extensive resident reformatting
          software.

Output Capabilities: 16mm microfilm cine or comic, one or
          two microimages per frame; 105mm microfiche, vertical,
          horizontal, or zig-zag pagination; standard or special
          formats; 24X, 42X, 48X.

Typography: Gothic type face only; standard set of ninety
        alphanumerics includes upper and lower case
        alphabet; special symbols available to customer
        order; two character sizes, selected by switch;
        larger size enlarges normal characters by fifteen
        percent; two character intensities: normal and
        boldface.

Page Formatting: sixty-four or eighty-six lines per page;
        up to 160 characters per line.

Retrieval Coding: image count marks, code-lines, MIRAcode
        (optional).

Special Features: will accept tapes formatted for IBM 1403
        line printers or Datagraphix COM recorders.

CAL COMP 1675

Vendor: California Computer Products, Inc.
         2411 West LaPalma
         Anaheim, California 92801

General Description: The Cal Comp 1675 is a high resolution
         COM recorder capable of alphanumeric or graphic
         output in an on-line or off-line environment.

Recording Method and Speed: CRT, stroke generation; rated
         speed (alphanumeric) is 15,000 lines per minute;
         typical throughput is 7,000 lines per minute.

Input Requirements: On-line operation to IBM 360/370 computers;
         EBCDIC code required; off-line operation from
         seven or nine track, NRZ or PE tapes, recorded at
         200, 556, 800 or 1600 bits per inch; EBCDIC, ASCII,
         of BCD codes accepted.

Software Support: callable subroutines and print-tape
         translators available for alphanumeric applications;
         extensive graphics software library available for
         contour plotting, mapping, graphing, flowchart
         generation, network display, and special requirements.

Output Capabilities: 16mm and 35mm microfilm cine or comic
         mode; 105mm microfiche; 15X, 42X, 48X.

Typography: standard sixty-four character set created by
         stroke generation from stored character definitions;
         unlimited extensions possible through software;
         OCR-B type face; one size and intensity standard;
         twenty intensity levels available; character size
         infinitely variable through software.

Page Formatting: up to eighty-eight lines per page, 160
         characters per line.

Retrieval Coding: image count marks; MIRAcode (optional).

CAL COMP 2100 SERIES (7 Models)

Vendor: California Computer Products, Inc.
          2411 West La Palma
          Anaheim, California 92801

General Description: The Cal Comp 2100 Series is a group
          of seven alphanumeric COM recorders. Models
          2130 and 2131 are on-line devices capable of
          producing 16mm roll microfilm and 105mm microfiche
          respectively. Models 2140 and 2141 are intended
          for previous Cal Comp customers who already own
          a Cal Comp 900, 915, or 925 Controller. Models
          2150 and 2151 are designed for new customers and
          include a Cal Comp 925 Controller, with 8K bytes
          of core, and a tape drive. The Microfiche
          Management System (MMS) consists of a 2151 recorder
          with a 925 Controller with additional core, and
          microfiche formatting software.

Recording Method and Speed: CRT, stroke generation; rated
          speed is 18,000 lines per minute; typical throughout
          is in the range 10,000 or 15,000 lines per minute.

Input Requirements: Models 2130 and 2131 operate on-line
          to IBM 360/30, 370/135, and larger IBM computers;
          EBCDIC code is required. For Models 2140, 2141,
          2150, and 2151, customers select from several
          available type drives including seven track NRZ,
          nine track NRZ or PE, or a universal drive.
          EBCDIC is standard system code. MMS or other
          system software permits translation of ASCII, BCD
          or other codes.

Software Support: Model 2130 emulates IBM 1403 or equivalent
          line printer; callable subroutines are used to
          create titled, indexed microfiche with Model 2131;
          callable subroutines and print-tape translators
          available for Models 2140, 2141, 2150, and 2151.
          Microfiche Management System (MMS) includes extensive
          resident fiche formatting software.

Output Capabilities: Models 2130, 2140, and 2150 produce
          16mm roll microfilm, cine or comic mode, 24X;
          Models 2131, 2141, and 2151 produce 105mm
          microfiche; vertical pagination; 24X, 42X, 48X;
          optional 16mm adapter kit available.

Typography: sixty-four character set standard; entended 136
          character set includes diacritical marks, European
          characters, and special symbols, Katakana character
          set available; one character size and intensity;
          OCR-B type face.

Page Formatting: sixty-four lines per page, 132 characters
          per line standard; MMS permits seventy-two lines
          per page, 136 characters per line.

Retrieval Coding: image count marks.

DATAGRAPHIX 4200

Vendor: Stromberg-DatagraphiX, Inc.
          P.O. Box 82449
          San Diego, California   92112

General Description: The DatagraphiX 4200 is an alphanumeric
          COM recorder capable of on-line operation to IBM
          360/370 computers. The 4200 is no longer in
          production and has been replaced by the model 4520
          in the DatagraphiX COM recorder line.

Recording Method and Speed: CRT, Charactron Shaped Beam Tube;
          rated speed is 15,000 lines per minute.

Input Requirements: operates on-line to IBM 360, model 25
          and above or and IBM 370; EBCDIC code required.

Software Support: callable subroutines available for fiche
          titling and indexing.

Output Capabilities: 16mm roll microfilm simplex or two-up
          formats; 35mm roll microfilm up to five microimages
          per frame; 82.5mm or 105mm microfiche in several
          formats; 25X, 42X, 48X.

Typography: sixty-four character set only; sans serif type
          face; one character size and intensity.

Page Formatting: sixty-four lines per page; up to 132
          characters per line.

Retrieval Coding: image count marks.

DATAGRAPHIX 4360

Vendor: Stromberg-DatagraphiX, Inc.
          P.O. Box 82449
          San Diego, California 92112

General Description: The DatagraphiX is an off-line alpha-
          numeric COM recorder. The 4360 is no longer in
          production and has been replaced by the DatagraphiX
          4530.

Recording Method and Speed: CRT, Charactron Shaped Beam
          Tube; rated speed is 10,000 lines per minute.

Input Requirements: seven or none tracks, NRZ or PE tapes,
          recorded at 556, 800, or 1600 bits per inch;
          EBCDIC, ASCII, or BCD codes.

Software Support: callable subroutines and print-tape
          translators available.

Output Capabilities: 16mm roll microfilm standard, 35mm roll
          microfilm and 105mm microfiche optional; several
          film and fiche formats possible; 21X, 25X, 30X,
          42X, 48X.

Typography: sixty-four character set; sans serif type face;
          one character size and intensity.

Page Formatting: sixty-four lines per page, 132 characters
          per line.

Retrieval Coding: image count marks.

DATAGRAPHIX 4440

Vendor: Stromberg-DatagraphiX, Inc.
           P.O. Box 82449
           San Diego, California 92112

General Description: The DatagraphiX 4440 is an off-line
           alphanumeric COM recorder that is a faster, more
           powerful version of the DatagraphiX 4360. The
           4440 is no longer in production and has been
           replaced by the DatagraphiX 4540.

Recording Method and Speed: CRT, Charactron Shaped Beam
           Tube; rated speed is 20,000 lines per minute.

Input Requirements: seven or nine track, NRZ or PE tapes,
           recorded at 556, 800, or 1600 bits per inch;
           EBCDIC, ASCII, or BCD codes; optional interface
           permits on-line operation to IBM 360/370 computers.

Software Support: callable subroutines and print-tape
           translators available.

Output Capabilities: 16mm roll microfilm standard; 35mm
           roll microfilm or 105mm microfiche optional;
           several film and fiche formats possible, 25X,
           42X, 48X.

Typography: sixty-four character set standard; extended
           128 character set optional; sans serif type face;
           one character size and intensity.

Page Formatting: sixty-four or seventy-six lines per page;
           132 characters per line.

Retrieval Coding: image count marks; code-lines; MIRAcode
           (optional).

DATAGRAPHIX 4500 SERIES (5 Models)

Vendor: Stromberg-DatagraphiX, Inc.
          P.O. Box 82449
          San Diego, California 92112

General Description: The DatagraphiX 4500 Series is a group
          of five alphanumerical COM recorders. Model 4520
          operates on-line to IBM 360/370 computers. Model
          4530 is an off-line recorder. Model 4500 is a
          more powerful version of the 4530. Model 4550
          is a minicomputer-controlled recorder. Model
          4560 is a more powerful version of the 4550.

Recording Method and Speed: CRT, Charactron Shaped Beam
          Tube; rated speeds range from 14,000 to 20,000
          lines per minute.

Input Requirements: Model 4520 operates on-line to the
          IBM 360, model 25 and above, or any IBM 370;
          EBCDIC code is required; Models 4530, 4540,
          4550, and 4560 accept seven or nine track, NRZ
          or PE tapes, recorded at 556, 800, or 1600 bits
          per inch; EBCDIC, ASCII, or BCD codes.

Software Support: callable subroutines available for
          model 4520; callable subroutines and print-tape
          translators available for models 4530 and 4540.
          Models 4550 and 4560 utilize Lockheed SUE
          minicomputer as preprocessor with extensive
          resident reformatting software.

Output Capabilities: 16mm roll microfilm or 105mm microfiche;
          vertical or horizontal fiche pagination; 24X, 42X,
          48X.

Typography: sixty-four character set standard, expandable
          to 128, 160, or 190 characters; special symbols
          available; Katakana character set available;
          OCR-B type face; one character size; regular and
          boldface intensities.

Page Formatting: up to eighty lines per page; eighty, 132,
          144, or 160 characters per line.

Retrieval Coding: image count marks.

DATAGRAPHIX AUTO COM

Vendor: Stromberg-DatagraphiX, Inc.
         P.O. Box 82449
         San Diego, California 92112

General Description: The DatagraphiX Auto COM is a microfiche
         recorder/processor that exposes, develops, and
         delivers cut, dry microfiche from appropriately-
         formatted tapes in one continuous operation; on-line
         or off-line operation is possible.

Recording Method and Speed: CRT, Charactron Shaped Beam
         Tube; rated speed is 12,000 lines per minute.

Input Requirements: seven or nine track, NRZ or PE tapes,
         recorded at 556, 800, or 1600 bits per inch;
         EBCDIC or BCD codes.

Software Support: callable subroutines and print-tape
         translators available.

Output Capabilities: 105mm microfiche; developed, cut, and
         dry; vertical pagination; 42X or 48X.

Typography: 120 character set; special symbols available;
         OCR-B type face; one size and intensity.

Page Formatting: sixty-four or eighty lines per page; 132
         or 160 characters per line.

Retrieval Coding: none.

Special Features: integrated processor delivers cut, dry
         microfiche ready for viewing or duplication.

INFORMATION INTERNATIONAL FR-80 GRAPHIC RECORDER

Vendor: Information International
          5933 Slauson Avenue
          Culver City, California 90230

General Description: the Information FR-80 is a high-quality,
          off-line COM recorder with extensive alphanumeric and
          graphic capability. An internal minicomputer enables
          the FR-80 to accept tapes prepared for a wide range
          of line printers and other COM recorders.

Recording Method and Speed: CRT, stroke-generation; rated
          speed is 10,000 lines per minute (alphanumeric).

Input Requirements: choice of seven track, NRZ tapes recorded
          at 556 or 800 bits per inch; nine track, NRZ tapes
          recorded at 800 bits per inch; or nine track, PE
          tapes recorded at 1600 bits per inch; EBCDIC, ASCII, BCD.

Software Support: internal minicomputer with extensive resident
          reformatting software will accept tapes prepared by
          wide-range of general-purpose computers; special
          software available for text editing and composition.

Output Capabilities: 16mm, 35mm, and 70mm roll microfilm,
          perforated or unperforated; 105mm microfiche;
          105mm and 127mm unperforated film for large
          format recording; many possible formats; 24X,
          42X, 48X.

Typography: 128 character set standard, expandable to 242;
          three type faces standard, including OCR-B and NMA
          Microfont; optional Utility Publication Expansion
          option includes utility and graphic arts character
          generator; sixty-four character sizes; eight intensity
          levels standard, expandable to sixty-four or 256.

Page Formatting: many page formats possible.

Retrieval Coding: image count marks; code-lines; MIRAcode.

Special Features: Forms Design Language and Compiler permits
          stroking of form on CRT with data to user-specifications;
          optional full-color recording available.

KODAK KOM-80, MODELS 60, 90, and 120

Vendor: Eastman Kodak Company
          343 State Street
          Rochester, New York 14650

General Description: The Kodak KOM-80 is a high-speed,
          off-line alphanumeric COM recorder. Three models
          are available. Models 90 and 120 are minicomputer-
          controlled.

Recording Method and Speed: CRT, stroke-generation; rated
          speed is 27,000 lines per minute (Model 60)
          40,000 lines per minute (Model 90), and 54,000
          lines per minute (Model 120); typical throughput
          is 23,000 lines per minute.

Input Requirements: nine track NRZ or PE tapes recorded at
          800 or 1600 bits per inch; EBCDIC code required.

Software Support: for Model 60, extensive software library
          of callable subroutines and print-tape translators
          available; Models 90 and 120 utilize a Hewlett-
          Packard 2022B minicomputer with extensive resident
          reformatting software.

Output Capabilities: 16mm and 35mm roll microfilm; 82.5mm
          and 105mm microfiche; 23X, 24X, 28X, 42X, 48X;
          many formats possible.

Typography: sixty-four character set standard, optionally
          expandable to eighty-two; special symbols available
          to customer order; four type faces: regular, italic,
          bold, and bold italic, interchangeable within print
          lines; two intensities.

Page Formatting: sixty-four lines per page; 132 characters
          per line.

Retrieval Coding: image count marks, code-lines, MIRAcode
          (optional).

Special Features: Models 90 and 120 will accept tapes formatted
          for Kodak KOM-90 Recorder.

KODAK KOM-90

Vendor: Eastman Kodak Company
           343 State Street
           Rochester, New York 14650

General Description: The Kodak KOM-90 is a high-speed, off-line
           alphanumeric COM recorder. Although the KOM-90 is no
           longer being actively marketed, it remains in wide
           service bureau use.

Recording Method and Speed: CRT, stroke generation; rated
           speed is 40,000 lines per minute.

Input Requirements: IBM-compatible seven or nine track, NRZ
           or PE tapes, recorded at 200, 556, 800, or 1600 bits
           per inch; EBCDIC or BCD code required.

Software Support: extensive software library of callable
           subroutines and print-tape translators available.

Output Capabilities: 16mm and 35mm roll microfilm; 82.5
           and 105mm microfiche; 23X, 24X, 28X, 42X; many
           formats possible.

Typography: sixty-four character set, optionally expandable
           to 121; special symbols available; roman, bold,
           and italic type faces; two intensity levels.

Page Formatting: sixty-four lines per page, 132 characters
           per line.

Retrieval Coding: image count marks, code-lines, MIRAcode
           (optional).

KODAK KOMSTAR 100, 200, and 300

Vendor: Eastman Kodak Company
          343 State Street
          Rochester, New York 14650

General Description: The Kodak Komstar recorders are a recently-
          introduced group of laser beam recorders employing special
          dry processed silver halide microfilm. Models 100 and
          200 are designed for on-line operation to IBM System
          360/370 computers. Model 200 incorporates a mini-
          computer. Model 300 is a mini-computer controlled
          off-line recorder.

Recording Method and Speed: Laser Beam Recording; 7,000 to
          10,000 lines per minute throughput rate.

Input Requirements: nine track, PE tapes recorded at 1600
          bits per inch; various codes acceptable.

Software Support: extensive software library available for all
          models.

Output Capabilities: 105mm microfiche and 16mm roll microfilm;
          24X, 32X, 42X, and 48X reductions available; 72X and
          96X possible with optional reduced-size character
          matrix.

Typography: sixty-four character EBCDIC character set plus
          three unique characters; lower-case emulation possible
          with optional reduced-size character matrix.

Page Formatting: choice of 8.5 by 11 or 11 by 14 inch page
          images; 64 lines per page, 132 characters per line
          standard; up to 102 lines per page and 207 characters
          per line possible with optional reduced-size character
          matrix.

Retrieval Coding: image count marks.

Special Features: accepts tapes formatted for Kodak KOM-80
          and KOM-85 microfilmers.

MEMOREX 1603 COM PRINTER

Vendor: Memorex Corporation
          Equipment Group
          San Tomas at Central Expressway
          Santa Clara, California 95052

General Description: the Memorex 1603 is an on-line alphanumeric
          COM recorder designed as a high-speed line printer
          replacement.

Recording Method and Speed: Light-Emitting-Diodes, five by
          seven dot matrix; rated speed is 10,000 lines per
          minute.

Input Requirements: operates on-line to IBM 360/370 computers.

Software Support: not applicable; recorder is plug-compatible
          replacement for IBM 1403 and 1443 line printers.

Output Capabilities: 16mm roll microfilm, cine mode; 24X.

Typography: sixty-four character set; sans serif type face;
          one character size and intensity.

Page Formatting: sixty-four lines per page, 132 characters
          per line.

Retrieval Coding: none.

QUANTOR 105 and 115

Vendor: Quantor Corporation
           520 Logue Avenue
           Mountain View, California 94943

General Description: The Quantor 105 is an off-line alphanumeric
           COM recorder/processor that exposes, develops, and
           delivers cut, dry microfiche as one continuous operation.
           Throughput is approximately one titled, indexed micro-
           fiche per minute. The Quantor 115 is a minicomputer-
           controlled version of the 105.

Recording Method and Speed: CRT, using a seven by ten dot
           matrix; rated speed is 15,000 lines per minute;
           typical throughput is 10,000 lines per minute.

Input Requirements: for model 105, nine track NRZ tapes
           recorded at 800 bits per inch standard; optional
           universal or other tape drives available; model
           115 accepts seven or nine track NRZ or PE tapes
           recorded at 556, 800, or 1600 bits per inch;
           for model 105, EBCDIC code is standard; factory-
           installed ASCII, BCD, NCR, or other code translators
           available; model 115 pre-processor accepts EBCDIC,
           ASCII, BCD, NCR, or other codes.

Software Support: for model 105, callable subroutines and
           print-tape translator packages available; model
           115 uses NCR 606 as pre-processor with extensive
           resident reformatting software.

Output Capabilities: 105mm microfiche; vertical or horizontal
           pagination; 24X, 42X, 48X.

Typography: sixty-four character IBM PN print chain is
           standard; 128 character extended set optional;
           one character size and intensity; Japanese Katakana
           and special character sets available.

Page Formatting: sixty-four lines per page, 132 characters
           per line standard; eighty-six lines per page, 160
           characters per line optional; scrolling optional.

Retrieval Coding: none.

Special Features: integrated processor delivers cut, dry
           microfiche ready for viewing or duplication; normal
           or reversal processing possible; will accept tapes
           formatted for DatagraphiX and Pertec recorders.

3M BETA COM RECORDERS (Models 700S, 700H, 800)

Vendor: 3M Company
          Microfilm Products Division
          3M Center
          St. Paul, Minnesota 55101

General Description: The 3M Beta COM recorders are off-line
          minicomputer-controlled devices. Models 700S and
          700H are primarily alphanumeric units with business
          graphics capability. Model 800 is a high resolution
          graphic recorder. 3M acquired the Beta COM series
          from its original manufacturer, Gould Graphic Systems.
          the units were previously marketed as the Gould 600L,
          700L, and 800 Beta COM recorders.

Recording Method and Speed: CRT, seven by nine dot matrix in
          the 700S; CRT, stroke-generation in the 700H and 800;
          rated speed is 14,000 lines per minute for the 700S,
          lines per minute for the 800.

Input Requirements: seven or nine track, NRZ or PE tapes,
          recorded at 556, 800, or 1600 bits per inch; EBCDIC,
          ASCII, or BCD codes.

Software Support: all models use DEC PDP-8/E as preprocessor
          with extensive resident reformatting software; graphic
          software packages available.

Output Capabilities: 16mm and 35mm roll microfilm; 70mm or
          105mm microfiche in various formats; 12X, 18X, 24X,
          42X, 48X, 96X (model 800 only).

Typography: 129 character set standard; three character sizes;
          roman, boldface and italic type faces; four intensity
          levels in the 700S and 700H; eight intensity levels
          in the 800.

Page Formatting: seventy-nine lines per page, expandable to
          105; 132 characters per line, expandable to 160;
          proportional spacing, underlining, overlining,
          subscripting, superscripting, backspacing.

Retrieval Coding: image count marks, MIRAcode (optional).

3M SERIES F ELECTRON BEAM RECORDER (EBR)

Vendor: 3M Company
          Microfilm Products Division
          3M Center
          St. Paul, Minnesota 55101

General Description: the 3M EBR is an off-line alphanumeric
          COM recorder that deflects an electron beam to write
          characters directly onto 3M brand dry silver microfilm.
          An in-line processor develops exposed microimages
          through the application of heat.

Recording Method and Speed: Electron Beam Recording; rated
          speed is 20,000 lines per minute.

Input Requirements: seven or nine track, NRZ or PE tapes;
          200, 556, 800, or 1600 bits per inch; EBCDIC or
          BCD codes.

Software Support: extensive library of callable subroutines
          and print-tape translators available.

Output Capabilities: 16mm roll microfilm; one, two, or four
          microimages per frame; 25X, 42X, 48X, 52.5X.

Typography: sixty character set, expandable to 128 to include
          lower case alphabet and Greek mathematical symbols;
          sans serif type face; two character sizes; two
          intensity levels.

Page Formatting: variable frame advance and line lengths
          permit considerable format versatility in both comic
          and cine modes; sixty-four lines per page, 132
          characters per line the usual format; scrolling
          possible.

Retrieval Coding: image count marks.

Special Features: dry silver processor may be configured
          in-line or detached.

3M LASER BEAM RECORDING (LBR) SYSTEM

Vendor: 3M Company
          Microfilm Products Division
          3M Center
          St. Paul, Minnesota 55101

General Description: the 3M LBR System records characters on
          3M brand dry silver microfilm using a six milliwat
          helium-neon laser. An in-line processor develops
          exposed microimages through the application of heat.

Recording Method and Speed: Laser Beam Recording; rated speed
          is 8,000 lines per minute.

Input Requirements: seven or nine track, NRZ or PE tapes,
          recorded at 200, 556, 800, or 1600 bits per inch;
          EBCDIC, ASCII, and BCD codes standard; custom codes
          available.

Software Support: callable subroutines and print-tape
          translators available.

Output Capabilities: 16mm roll microfilm, cine or comic
          mode; 105mm microfiche, vertical pagination;
          25X, 42X, 48X.

Typography: sixty-four character set, expandable to 128;
          special symbols available; sans serif type face;
          one character size and intensity.

Page Formatting: sixty-four or eighty lines per page; 132
          or 136 characters per line.

Retrieval Coding: image count marks.

Special Features: dry silver processor may be configured
          in-line or detached; as an option, LBR can be
          operated on-line to an IBM 360/370 computer or
          interfaced with a minicomputer.

APPENDIX C

SELECTED STANDARDS RELEVANT TO COM RECORDING

NMA Industry Standards

MS1-1971   Quality Standards for Computer Output Microfilm

MS2-1976   Format and Coding for Computer Output Microfilm

MS8-1974   Document Mark (Blip) Used in Image Mark Retrieval Systems

MS104-1972   Recommended Practice for Inspection and Quality Control of First Generation Silver Halide Microfilm

MS108-1973   Microfiche Grid Gauge, 270 Frame, 48X

American National Standards

PH1.28-1973   Photographic Film for Archival Records, Silver-Gelatin Type, on Cellulose Ester Base, Specifications for

PH1.41-1973   Photographic Film for Archival Records, Silver-Gelatin Type, on Polyester Base, Specifications for

PH4.8-1971   Methylene Blue Method for Measuring Thiosulfate, and Silver Densitometric Method for Measuring Residual Chemicals in Films, Papers, and Plates

PH5.1-1970   Microfilm Readers for 16mm and 35mm Film on Reels, Specifications for

DOD Standards

MIL-F-80242   Film, Microfiche, 48X

MIL-V-80240A   Viewer Microfiche (24X and 48X)

MIL-V-80241   Viewer/Printer Microfiche (48X)

ISO Standards

ISO2803-1974   Archival Microfilm

ISO2707-1973   Transparent A6 Size Microfiche of Uniform Division

Other

ECMA-11   European Computer Manufacturers Association
Standard for the Alphanumeric Character Set
OCR-B for Optical Recognition

APPENDIX D

COMPANIES SPECIALIZING IN THE PRODUCTION OF COM CATALOGS

FOR LIBRARIES

Autographics, Inc.
751 Monterey Pass Rd.
Monterey, California
91754

Brodart, Inc.
1609 Memorial Ave.
Williamsport, Pennsylvania
17701

Library Interface Systems, Inc.
1421 Wayzata Blvd.
Wayzata, Minnesota
55391

Blackwell/North America
10030 S.W. Allen Blvd.
Beaverton, Oregon
97005

Inforonics
550 Newtown Rd.
Littleton, Massachusetts
01460

Science Press
Box 342
Herndon, Virginia
22070

APPENDIX E

SELECTED ADDITIONAL BIBLIOGRAPHY

186

Aaron, Clyde H. "Retrieval Techniques -- Flexibility for the Analyst," Proceedings of the National Microfilm Association 23 (1974): II-24-30.

Adelstein, P.Z. "A Progress Report: ANSI Activities on Stability of Processed Diazo and Vesicular Films," Journal of Micrographics 9 (1976): 99-101.

Airhart, Truett. "Computer Output Microfilm: a Powerful Systems Tool," Journal of Micrographics 7 (1974): 99-105.

Antal, J.R. "A Potential Buyer Looks at COM," Journal of Micrographics 3 (1969): 79-84.

Aschenborn, H.J. "UNICAT -- the South African Joint Catalogue of Monographs on Microfiche," Microdoc 11 (1972): 76-8.

Avedon, Don M. "Fundamentals of COM," Proceedings of the National Microfilm Association 22 (1973): II-83-88.

_____. "Proposed ISO Standard 'Computer Output Microfiche,'" Journal of Micrographics 9 (1976): 309-14.

Auerbach Publishers. Auerbach on Digital Plotters and Image Digitizers. (Philadelphia: Auerbach Publishers, Inc., 1972).

Beeman, Donald R. "Micrographic Standards for Containers (Cartridge and Cassette) for 16mm Roll Microfilm," Journal of Micrographics 9 (1975): 51-4.

Bierman, Kenneth John. "Automated Alternatives to Card Catalogs: the Current State of Planning and Implementation," Journal of Library Automation 8 (1975): 277-98.

Blue, Roger E. "Why a COM Service Bureau," Proceedings of the National Microfilm Association 24 (1975): 175-8.

Buckle, David. "The Cost of a COM Catalogue System at Birmingham University Library," Microdoc 13 (1974): 15-18.

Buckle, David and French, Thomas. "The Application of Microform to Manual and Machine-Readable Catalogues," Program 5 (1971): 41-66.

Burnham, Dwight C. and Hernon, James A. "COM Applications and Future Trends," Proceedings of the National Microfilm Association 22 (1973): II-186-219.

Butler, Brett and Van Pelt, John. "Microphotocomposition -- a
New Publishing Resource," Journal of Micrographics 6 (1972):
7-13.

Clarke, Alfred. "ABC's of COM," Journal of Micrographics 5
(1972): 205-6.

Collins, William H. "Recent Developments in Rear Projection
Screens," Journal of Micrographics 4 (1971): 201-7.

Corya, William L. "The Integration of Formats to Provide
Catalog Access Services," in Spigai, Frances, ed.,
Information Roundup: Proceedings of the Fourth ASIS
Mid-Year Meeting (Washington: American Society for
Information Science, 1975), 96-104.

Croissette, Jill C. Le. "Microfilm Catalogs in a British
Public Library System," Microform Review 4 (1975): 104-7.

Elrod, J. McRee. "Is the Card Catalogue's Unquestioned Sway
in North America Ending?," Journal of Academic Librarianship
2 (1976): 4-8.

Francis, B. and Phillips, C.M. "MICROCAT -- a Very Short Entry
Catalogue," Program 8 (1974): 22-28.

Freund, Clare E. "Catalog on Microfiche at the Eastman Kodak
Libraries," Special Libraries 68 (1977): 375-82.

Glickman, Stuart P. and Levine, Emil H. "Use of Microform in
Federal Narcotics Intelligence and Law Enforcement," Journal
of Micrographics 9 (1976): 155-9.

Grausnick, Robert P. and Kottenstette, James. A Performance
Evaluation: Microfiche vs. Hardcopy (Denver: Denver
Research Institute, 1971).

Grausnick, Robert P. and Kottenstette, James. An Investigation
of the Environment for Educational Microform Utilization
(Denver: Denver Research Institute, 1971).

Harmon, George H. "A Service Bureau -- How to Select One,"
Journal of Micrographics 8 (1975): 135-7.

Jeske, Roy. "COM Cameras," Journal of Micrographics 4 (1971):
275-81.

Johnson, R.W. et al. Multi Coded Microfilm Feasibility Study
(Dover, N.J.: Picatinny Arsenal, 1975).

Kingett, A.E. "COM: an Assessment," Microdoc 10 (1971): 50-7.

Knight, Nancy H. "Microform Catalog Data Retrieval Systems: a Survey," Library Technology Reports (Chicago: American Library Association, 1975).

Kruger, Lester O. "Why 'They' Don't Make Microform Machines for Libraries," South African Libraries 43 (1975): 25-6.

MacLeod, I.M. "COM with a Difference," Microdoc 15 (1976): 4-9.

Martin, Susan K. "Mixed Media for a Serial System: Hardcopy, Microform, and CRT's," in Spigai, Frances, ed., Information Roundup: Proceedings of the Fourth ASIS Mid-Year Conference (Washington: American Society for Information Science, 1975), pp. 111-117.

Massie, James G. and Smink, Jay. "COM Operations -- Is COM a Better Way?," Proceedings of the National Microfilm Association 22 (1973): II-164-176.

Metzger, James and Callaghan, William. "Duplicating Third Generation 48X COM Output on Vesicular Film for Large Scale Distribution: Problems and Quality Control," in Chenevert, Don, ed., Micrographics Science 1973: Winter Symposium (Washington: Society of Photographic Scientists and Engineers, 1973), pp. 133-6.

Miller, Roger C. "Why Don't They Make Microform Machines for Libraries?," Microform Review 2 (1973): 91-2.

Nache, Otto. "An Integrated Micro-Information System Taking Industrial Medicine as a Model," Proceedings of the Special Libraries Association, Sixty-Seventh Annual Conference, New York City, June 6-10, 1976.

Robertson, John R. "A Rational Approach to COM," Journal of Micrographics 3 (1969): 73-7.

Robinson, F. "The Uses of OCR and COM in Information Work," Program 8 (1974): 137-48.

Schieber, Larry. "Photocomposition on a COM Recorder," Journal of Micrographics 8 (1975): 251-4.

Smith, G.W. "Diazo for Microfilm," Microdoc 10 (1971): 2-4.

Smith, Robert Judd. "Microfiche Indexing Systems," Proceedings of the National Microfilm Association 24 (1975): 244-53.

Smitzer, L.A. "The Art of Roll Film Look-Up," <u>Proceedings of the National Microfilm Association</u> 17 (1968): 57-61.

Smock, Sidney N. "Microfiche Poison Index and Management Saves Lives," <u>Journal of Micrographics</u> 8 (1975): 127-30.

Teplitz, Arthur. "The Design of Microfiche Systems," <u>Human Factors</u> 12 (1970): 225-30.